HOME COURT ADVANTAGE

FOCUS ON THE FAMILY
RESOURCES

HOME COURT ADVANTAGE

Preparing Your
Children
to Be
Winners
in Life

Dr. Kevin Leman

TYNDALE

Tyndale House Publishers
Wheaton, Illinois

Home Court Advantage
Copyright © 2005 by Dr. Kevin Leman
All rights reserved. International copyright secured.

A Focus on the Family book published by
Tyndale House Publishers, Wheaton, Illinois 60189

TYNDALE is a registered trademark of Tyndale House Publishers, Inc. Tyndale's quill logo is a trademark of Tyndale House Publishers, Inc.

All Scripture quotations, unless otherwise indicated, are taken from the *Holy Bible, New International Version* ®. NIV ®. Copyright 1973, 1978, 1984 by the International Bible Society. Used by permission of Zondervan Publishing House. All rights reserved.

No part of this publication may be reproduced, stored in a retrieval system, or transmitted in any form or by any means—electronic, mechanical, photocopy, recording, or otherwise—without prior permission of Focus on the Family.

Focus on the Family books are available at special quantity discounts when purchased in bulk by corporations, organizations, churches, or groups. Special imprints, messages, and excerpts can be produced to meet your needs. For more information, contact: Focus on the Family, 8605 Explorer Drive, Colorado Springs, CO 80920; or phone (800) 932-9123.

Cover Design: Brian Merculief
Cover Photography: Efrain Garcia
Cover Copy: Joy Olson

Library of Congress Cataloging-in-Publication Data
Leman, Kevin.
Home court advantage: preparing your children to be winners in life / Kevin Leman.
   p. cm.
At head of title: Focus on the Family.
Includes bibliographical references.
ISBN 1-58997-207-4
1. Family—Religious life. 2. Parenting—Religious aspects—Christianity. I. Title.
BV4526. 3.L46 2005
248.8'45—dc22

                    2004028680

Printed in the United States of America

05 06 07 08 09 10 11/10 9 8 7 6 5 4 3 2 1

This book is affectionately dedicated to my wife of 38 years, Sande.

You have surely made our house a home and have certainly been the major part in giving our kids the home court advantage.

Contents

PART 1

HOME IS WHERE THE HEART IS

You Can't Have It All

Defining the Problem

I f Kevin Leman is in the air, two things are probably true. First, he's sitting in the front row. I get a bit claustrophobic, and after flying over three million miles, it's the least my airline can do to allow me a little extra space.

Second, the words "American Airlines" are painted on the tin can I'm flying on. I've been a frequent flyer with American since 1988. Early on, I flew other airlines as well, but now, as long as American can accommodate me, I'm pretty loyal to this one airline.

Why?

It's all about the "home court advantage." Irregular flyers can sign up for the frequent flyer program, but they get credited with their actual miles. Me? I get *double miles* wherever I go, which adds up pretty fast. Plus, on occasion I get free upgrades—even free tickets!

And when my schedule changes, American goes out of its way to please me. You might get to the airport three hours before I do to get your name on the standby list in hopes of catching an earlier flight. I might show up just 30 minutes before the plane pushes back, but I'm the one who gets the seat. Why? With over 3,000,000 miles in my account, I'm what they call a "Lifetime Platinum" member, which is airline-speak for "Please this sucker at all costs, because he's spent enough on plane tickets over the years to buy the plane he's flying on."

In short, when I'm flying American, I have a distinct advantage. If I step onto a United flight, or a Northwest flight, or a Southwest flight, I'm Joe Schmo. I'll get the same packet of peanuts as everyone else. Some other lug will get the good seat up front. And I might even be stuck in a middle seat, which at my age and size feels like a rhinoceros being crammed into Tweety Bird's cage.

It's a nice feeling, living life on American Airlines as a Lifetime Platinum member.

Wouldn't you like to give your kids the same sense of security and joy and even happiness? Wouldn't you like them to feel that being born into your family has given them something special? Wouldn't you like them to be as loyal to you as I am to American?

Well, that can happen if you'll learn the magic of creating the "home court advantage."

A sports team gains significant advantage while playing on the home court, where its greatest fans cheer it on and create an energy that can mean the difference between loss and victory. It's the same with your family. A home court advantage comes from seeing home as a place of security, joy, and memories. It means the best part of a kid's life will come from what happens within the four walls of that blessed place spelled H-O-M-E. It means his or her parents won't let the outside world with all its enticements and opportunities take that child away from the place that matters more than anyplace else.

This book is all about giving your child the home court advantage.

Besting Your Best

Charlie's mother wanted the best for her 12-year-old son. He already took piano lessons, but Mom wanted to broaden his experience. When she found a wonderful instructor to train him on the violin—a man who would nurture her son's love of the instrument and encourage his gifts—she was ecstatic.

But music wasn't all that occupied Charlie's time. Every Saturday he attended enrichment classes to supplement his Monday through Friday schooling. During the summer he took an S.A.T. prep class at the university to give him an extra edge for the college placement test four years down the road.

Charlie loved the violin, but hated his mother's expectations. "*Mom*," he would complain when his mother criticized his technique, "I just want to play!"

Charlie wasn't the only one in his class who felt the pressure to perform. Another student's mother was so critical during lessons that the instructor had to ask the woman to remain outside so the young musician could concentrate. Still another student, only nine years old, was performing three times a week with the metropolitan ballet company's production of "The Nutcracker," training for gymnastics twice a week, and attending a Brownie meeting every other week. Her mother had bought the girl a Day-Timer to juggle homework and activities.

After a month, however, Charlie finally got a break—in a manner of speaking. Despite the boy's love for the violin, his mother pulled him out of lessons.

The reason? Her son didn't bring home enough homework, she said. The instructor just wasn't pushing him hard enough.

You may think Charlie's mother crossed the line. But if you're like most parents, you want the best for your child, too—the best schools, teachers, and neighborhood. You want your son to succeed in his second grade reading class, and your daughter to excel in after-school gymnastics. This desire is as natural as the wonder you felt when she first entered the world, and as common as the apprehension you sometimes feel about doing your best as a parent. Any dad or mom with an ounce of love wants the best for his or her child.

But if you're also like many parents today, in spite of your intentions, you may not be giving your children what *is* best for them.

What's best, you ask? A steady diet of Mozart in the womb? Harvard-educated English tutors? One-on-one pointers from a Russian gymnastics coach?

No. I'm talking about the *best* thing, the most important thing, the thing that trumps placement on the state champion traveling soccer team or a full-ride scholarship to summer tuba camp. I'm talking about the foundation upon which security and stability are built in your children: Time together. At home. As a family.

Oh, come on, Dr. Leman, you may think, *get with the program.*

The program today, fellow parent, *is* the problem. In a society frenzied with activity, time together at home is more important than ever. In our efforts to help children "get ahead," we're bypassing the most important factor of their development—leisurely love and gracious attention at home in a hurried and harried world.

Please think about that phrase, "leisurely love." I've talked to thousands of children, and one thing has come through crystal clear in our conversations: "Rushed" love doesn't feel like love to a child. If your child feels like he's "on the clock," or if she thinks she's always interrupting you, *love* won't be the first word that comes to her mind when she thinks back on her childhood.

So much competes with time together at home as a family. The

Baskin Robbins of Life doesn't just offer activities in 31 flavors—it offers 31,000, and parents drool over the options like kids at an ice cream counter. You can shell out hundreds of dollars for your seven-year-old daughter to perfect her tee-ball swing with a former major league coach. You can arrange for your three-year-old son to begin working aggressively toward his judo black belt so he can shoulder-throw bullies in the preschool lunch line. You can hire a Metropolitan Opera star to give voice lessons to your kindergartner.

Activities, however, really are like ice cream: They may suffice for an occasional treat, but they don't make for a healthy diet. Those standing behind the counter might have you believe that all your little Einstein needs is the right combination of flavors to help him construct a unified quantum theory by the time he hits puberty. If you're like many parents, you may end up ordering a cone of activities piled so high you can't possibly handle all those scoops. When that happens, you've fallen victim to the lure of overparenting.

Overparenting: Don't Push It

A mother called an Atlanta physical therapy clinic, anxious to squeeze in an appointment. Her nine-year-old daughter had injured her arm swimming six times a week for two swim clubs. Now she was having trouble even lifting that arm.

The physical therapist made room for her in his schedule that afternoon. He grew concerned when a quick examination revealed that the girl, who was also involved in competitive soccer, couldn't raise her arm without significant pain.

"She really needs to rest this arm," the therapist advised.

"But the district championships are in 10 days!" Mom said.

"That may be so, but she needs to take at least one week off—a full seven days, and then we can reevaluate her. She's overworked this arm and needs to lay off."

"You don't understand," the mother argued. "It's the *district* championship. She's a *great* swimmer. She has such potential!"

Everywhere I go, parents like that mom want their kids to win. They want them to rise above the competition, finish first, and stand out.

Winning isn't bad. I don't go to the University of Arizona Wildcats basketball games to admire the team logo painted at center court. I *love* it when my team wins. But if it loses in the final 1.3 seconds on a brilliant three-point play by the opposing team, I won't turn to my youngest daughter and say, "Lauren, let's go tip and burn a police car, and maybe finish the evening throwing a few garbage cans through local business windows. What do you think?" Winning is good—in proper perspective.

But what difference is missing a couple weeks of swimming practice and a district meet going to make in the "swimming career" of a nine-year-old girl? Is she really going to miss the NCAA Swimming and Diving Championship ten years down the road because she didn't compete for four days in July? More to the point, why is this mother concerned about swimming stardom for her nine-year-old in the first place? When Proverbs, that age-old book of wisdom, says, "Train a child in the way he should go,"[1] it isn't talking about daily 5 A.M. laps in the pool.

High parental expectations are nothing new, but greater disposable time and income now allow us to pursue pie-in-the-sky dreams to a degree perhaps never seen before. Parents are throwing time and money at their kids' future "success" as if parenting were career coaching and family life were training for the Olympics.

I realize that most of you aren't packing your bags for the Olympic training facility in Colorado Springs. But if you step back and evaluate your expectations, you'll probably find that in some ways you *are* packing your child's emotional bags for that destination the world calls success.

Who knows? you think as your 18-month-old son picks up his little plastic golf putter and swings aimlessly at his little plastic golf ball. *He could be the next Tiger Woods.*

He may—though the odds are about a billion to one against it. But stare at that tiny glimmer of a thought too intently and it can slowly pollute your priorities. The PGA Tour is among the furthest things from your toddler's mind. That fantasy belongs to someone else—you, the parent, who may be trying to live out your dreams through your children.

These dreams need not be grandiose; often those that work their way most insidiously into a family's daily activities are the subtle assumptions. For example, you and your spouse, both teachers, may not expect your child to follow your career path; you may even be careful to let him choose his own vocation. But because both of you were once straight-A students, you may expect the same from your child whether he's going into theater management or biophysics research. What happens when you discover that your little Norbert is not an Albright scholar—that in fact, he's neither a scholar nor all that bright?

Or perhaps your high school plastered the gym wall with plaques of your all-star record-breaking feats. Your competitive streak may show from the soccer field sidelines as you yell for your elementary school daughter to "Go for the ball!" when all she wants to do is stand at midfield and talk with friends about the new student in class.

Such underlying expectations are hard to recognize in ourselves; it's easy to assume that what came naturally to us will come naturally to our own flesh and blood. And it's easy to push kids into all sorts of activities to get ahead.

The *activity trap*, I call it. It's not easy to escape, because you don't feel steel jaws biting into your leg when you're in it. More likely, your entrapment will be applauded. You may receive the praise of parents in your neighborhood carpool and believe you're helping your child advance. But if your family relationships and your child's character development are more important to you than whether he makes a career of hitting a little white ball long distances or is admitted to East Coast schools that are overgrown with ivy, then you need to examine how these misconceptions subtly affect *you*.

Conflict of Interest

"My daughter has such potential."

"We want to help our son get ahead."

"We're giving our kids the opportunities we never had."

These statements sound self-sacrificing, noble—even loving. If you've been saying them, no doubt you're doing so with good intentions. But examine your motives closely, for you may be pushing your child for your own good rather than hers.

Many parents today are like mountain climbing guides who drive their little clients to summits rising in their own imaginations. These moms and dads expose their kids to the fierce winds of competition and exhaust them in the process.

Ironically, many parents contend that such help benefits the child, enabling him to succeed and bolstering confidence. After all, the child is the one who'll apply for college six years down the road; better beef up that sixth grade résumé. The child is the one who'll face a fiercely competitive job market; better develop a track record starting with impeccable second grade 4-H club projects.

But is the child really the one who benefits?

"That's Wilhelmina's painting?" you hear during open house, "Oh, you must be so proud!" The praise feels so good you don't mention that you helped Wilhelmina choose her subject matter, mix the colors, and add a few, key touch-ups to bring the composition together.

"Your boy sure can throw a football!" a fellow dad confides to you along the sidelines at Saturday morning's game. In reality your son *hates* football and the father-son practices you've come to make him do.

Your daughter's report card reads, "Beatrice is a pleasure to have in class." The teacher doesn't know about the exhausting hours you and little Beatrice spend turning the family room into night school. Keep that up and soon Beatrice won't be a pleasure to have at school, home, or anywhere else!

Eventually, these kids may quit developing their own strengths to overcome obstacles and simply let their parents drag them along until they turn 18—and give up on themselves altogether.

I sometimes joke about visiting a school's science fair to search for a project that was done by the child himself. I can imagine the parents exclaiming the night before, "Would you turn that TV down? I'm trying to do your homework!" It's as if some moms and dads feel they're being graded themselves, hoping for a report card like this to post on the refrigerator: "Mr. and Mrs. Beasley are an absolute delight to have outside class! A+++!"

It's easy to feed off the positive strokes we get when we're stuck in the activity trap; people assume we must be great parents. But the consequences of our expectations can push our children out of the nest far too early.

No Worm for the Too-early Bird

"The sooner [children] are stimulated, the more they'll learn in the long run," says one mother who "tries to collect every video made by the Baby Einstein Co." Hers is a notion held by many parents, who by hoping "to boost their infants' and toddlers' IQ levels have made the brain-development niche one of the toy industry's strongest sectors since 2000, according to the Toy Industry Association."[2]

Some parents, not wanting their kids to be left behind in anything, push them to get ahead in everything. Believing the early bird gets the worm, they may think that bird must try its wings earlier and earlier to reach the head of the pecking order. Thus the early childhood years, which should be a time of bonding between parent and child, are transformed into a survival-of-the-fittest battle among the little peeps.

This push to give young kids a head start begins subtly, when parents compare their children's vocabulary, make mental notes on who's still in diapers and who's graduated to the toilet, and assess who can finger-paint the best impressionistic rainbow in the neighborhood play group. Before long you might find yourself thinking, *No doubt about it—the Carsons' kid is ahead of ours.* When children are piloting cross-country in Cessna airplanes at the ages of seven and eight[3], it's easy to feel your hatchlings are lagging behind.

But have you ever watched a nest of baby birds? The strongest hatchling, the one who often ventures into the world first, isn't always the most successful. In fact, if it leaves the nest too soon, it may not survive the first few weeks. Even if your kids get an early start, it doesn't always have the intended effect.

You've probably heard of the famous 1993 study by Rauscher, Shaw, and Ky regarding the so-called "Mozart effect." It suggested that children who listened to classical music while they were very young developed higher IQs than those who didn't. The findings became so popular that in 1998 the governor of Georgia, Zell Miller, began giving classical music CDs to every child born in the state.

But independent studies have since shown that the Mozart effect doesn't exist. Today, developmental psychologists say the best way to stimulate a youngster's brain is through multisensory input. " 'Babies learn through multiple senses being rewarded simultaneously,' says Irving Lazar, a developmental psychologist and professor emeritus at Cornell University. 'This means the best opportunity for a child to learn is from another person,' who can stimulate sight, sound, taste, touch, and smell, sometimes all at once."[4]

Many parents still use the "baby genius" videos, thinking, *Well, they can't hurt.* But Lazar and Lisa Bain, editor of *Parenting* magazine, caution that filling toddlers' time with such screen-staring can remove the foundation of their development—human interaction.

"Flashcards for an infant?" asked one toy store manager, who refused to carry them. "I can't imagine flashing cards at a 6-month-old. Take them for a walk. Let them see a real flower."[5]

In short, social interaction rather than intellectual exercises is what nurtures your child's development. And what more important social interaction is there than that within the family?

It's easy to defer to the so-called experts and marketers who'd have you believe that their products are integral to your baby's development. But if you want to have a homegrown child, raising your kid isn't something a TV set—or a stranger—can do.

Making an Indelible Imprint

Dr. Brenda Hunter, psychologist and author, describes what I call the "indelible imprint" that a parent leaves on a child. She believes that the parental relationship forms the basis for a child's perceptions of himself or herself. "According to Bowlby," she says in her book *Home by Choice*, "a young child forms 'internal working models' of himself, his parental attachments, and his world out of the raw material of his parental relationships. Based on the way his parents treat him, a child will form certain expectations about how others will treat him. If the parents are warm, loving, and emotionally accessible, the child comes to believe that *he* is loving and worthy. As he matures, he will possess high self-esteem; he will be able to trust others and, later in life, have the capacity to be intimate with a spouse and children. Secure in his parental attachments, this individual will expect others to treat him the same way his parents have."[6]

Those raw materials include your physical affection, your presence at home, and your spoken words to your child. The child whose introduction to language from her parents includes hearing that she "doesn't amount to much" will soon come to believe what she hears. Conversely, the child whose introduction to the world through language is shaped by consistent affirmations that she is loved will form a mental image of herself that fits those messages.

Before you read any further—*stop!* Do you understand what Dr. Hunter is pointing out here? Slowly reread those two paragraphs above—out loud even—because they are *so* crucial to our discussion of setting up the home court advantage and leaving that indelible imprint on your children.

The Lights Are On, But No One's Home

Unfortunately, some parents aren't passing many messages to their kids at all. No doubt you've heard of the study showing that, on average, fathers communicate with their teenage children just 35 minutes per week.[7] Thirty-five minutes! I spend more time than that picking lint from my belly button. And it isn't just fathers who are absent from their children's lives. Another study, published in *Time* magazine, found that "72% of women with children under 18 are in the work force—a figure that is up sharply from 47% in 1975."[8] The reasons for parents' absence may be complex, but the bottom line is that they *are* absent.

I realize that some may have legitimate reasons for not having a parent at home with the children. As that same issue of *Time* magazine stated, "Since the mid-'70s, the amount of the average family budget earmarked for the mortgage has increased a whopping 69% (adjusted for inflation). At the same time, the average father's income increased less than 1%."[9] Often, Mom picks up the slack by jumping into the marketplace.

But many of the families I see as I travel throughout the country have their children in child care for other reasons. It's not because they have no options, such as enlisting family or co-op child care, or adopting a less expensive standard of living. It's because they have other priorities: climbing the corporate ladder or keeping up with the Joneses. Many parents use child care to stay in the rat race, or don't even consider whether Dad or Mom might be able to stay at home even part time. That's tragic, when the most important thing you can give your children is your presence—more important than a better house in a better neighborhood in a better school district.

But aren't we supposed to be able to "have it all"? Isn't it the American dream to have a new house, two kids, two cars, and two upwardly mobile jobs?

If funding those car and mortgage payments takes needed time away from your child, it doesn't matter how great the *house* looks if the *home* inside isn't doing so hot. I know this isn't a popular thing to say, but when you hand your child over to day care, regardless of your motives, you're missing literally thousands of opportunities for positive imprinting. That missing piece is the most critical one. When it comes to establishing a homegrown relationship with your children, raising them at home for the first six years really is the best option.

Can day care give your child a safe place to play? Yes. Can it provide a positive place for social interaction? Yes. Can it provide a basis for a good education? Yes. Can it reinforce your values? If you choose your day care provider carefully, maybe.

Where day care fails is in nurturing a relationship with you. That's because you can't have homegrown kids without being regularly involved in their lives.

As you read this book, I want you to examine the time you spend away from home. *Why* do you do so? Is it really because you have to, or is it because you've embraced more opportunities than you can manage and have locked yourself into a tyrannical schedule? Consider how you might—and will—cut back to spend more time at home together as a family. No matter how much or how little time you have in the end, commit to making the most of what you have.

I understand that making time to be with your kids—especially keeping them home during the preschool years—takes sacrifice. My oldest daughter, Krissy, and her husband, Dennis, recently had their first child; they made the difficult decision for Krissy to stay at home. Because of that decision, they're just barely making it financially. But I believe that they—and you—can rise to the challenge.

"An August 2003 poll for the Center for a New American Dream, an organization based in Takoma Park, Md., that focuses on quality-of-life issues, revealed that although 60% of Americans felt pressure to work too much, more than 80% wished for more family time and that 52% of them would take less money to get it."[10] If that statistic is indeed representative, the fact that you're reading this book means you're probably among those willing to make the sacrifice to keep your children at home with you as much as possible. Will Krissy and Dennis have to reevaluate their decision? Perhaps. But they're giving it their best shot, committing to make the sacrifice, and then stretching to live in line with their priorities.

Is it worth it? My guess is that years down the road, for them the answer will be a *yes* more unequivocal than they feel even now—a *yes* from both them and their son, Connor. That's because kids really do garner a positive self-image and a sense of security by spending time with their parents in a loving environment.

Having a homegrown child—creating the home court advantage— is well worth the sacrifice.

What Is Homegrown?

Homegrown parenting and the home court advantage begin by looking forward. Years from now, when your daughter heads off to college or your son moves into his first apartment and you bid her or him farewell with teary eyes, what do you want your child to be able to handle? What kind of foundation would you like him or her to have?

A homegrown child isn't known by what she *does* as much as by what she *is*. That's an important distinction that can be developed only through time and parental involvement.

Maybe you've heard the parable of the wise man who built his house upon the rock and the foolish man who built his house upon the sand. Given the choice between the two, sand seems at first the way to go; certainly it's the path of least resistance. It's easier to sink pillars into sand than rock, sand is easy to level, and it usually comes with a great view of the ocean.

But even though a house on the beach might seem like a dream come true, it may be a nightmare in the making: storms and waves might wash away all that you've labored over the years to build. As you watch your house float out to sea, you may think twice about your choice of foundations—which is what I hope you'll do as you think about the foundation you want to build for your child.

Laying a firm foundation doesn't happen overnight. If you want a homegrown child—one who's nurtured at home by involved parents, who has downtime, who is raised for character and not just achievement, who values faith and family—you construct that foundation in layers, day by day.

But the work is worth it. The tremors of childhood and adolescence can shatter other, weaker foundations. A homegrown child will stand firm when she's ridiculed for having big ears, when he gets cut from the team, when her boyfriend breaks up with her and it feels that the ground beneath her is quaking.

A homegrown child has values and lives by them. He has the moxie to stick with it because you've given him Vitamin E—for Encouragement. She has the courage to say "No" because you've given her Vitamin N.

A homegrown child is different—from the inside out.

The Homegrown Difference

You may ask, "Does it matter? Can you really tell the difference?"

Well, let me ask you this: Have you ever eaten homegrown sweet corn?

A while back we had some people over for steaks cooked outside on the grill. My wife, Sande, is an excellent cook; the last thing she brought outside was a massive platter of hot corn on the cob, the steam curling into the air.

I love corn on the cob, so when I saw that plate I began salivating. I was remembering the corn we eat in western New York all summer long—so sweet you'd think someone had sprinkled sugar on it. After slathering a piece with butter and pelting it with salt, I started into it like a mad woodpecker.

By the time I reached the end of the first row, however, my face began to scrunch up. *This stuff's awful,* I thought. Though it looked like sweet corn, it was anything but!

If you think there's no difference between supermarket and homegrown sweet corn, compare what you get at your local grocery store with what's offered at a farm stand where they've picked the corn that morning. Your eye may not see a difference, but your taste buds will.

The same thing is true with children. Many kids may seem on the surface to be well-mannered and polite. Get past those exteriors, though, and you may find that they play by the rules but lack the inner core of their own convictions.

There's more to having homegrown children than simply cultivating certain behaviors. A homegrown kid is like that sweet corn—the secret lies inside. That's where a special relationship connects parent and child. What defines homegrown kids more than anything else is an authentic, carefully cultivated relationship with their parents. They have been nurtured with the home court advantage.

This book is all about that relationship. It's about embracing what matters most. It's about setting priorities that will help your family meet a standard of success that makes sense.

In the next few chapters, we'll identify myths that sidetrack many parents. In the second section, we'll look at raising kids from the inside out. Finally, because many parents replace the rat race outside the home with one inside, we'll consider practical tips for escaping the activity trap—even how to encourage family time together without driving your kids to hate it.

Creating the home court advantage is easier than you might think—especially when compared with trying to keep up with the Joneses, who never should have set the pace in the first place. Let's turn now to some of the ways we tend to forget a crucial truth—that there really is no place like home.

Let's Remember:

- Time together at home as a family is the foundation upon which security and stability are built in your children.
- Having a homegrown child is all about the relationship. Your relationship with your children—how you see and interact with them—forms the basis for their perceptions of themselves.
- You *can't* have it all. Ask yourself: *What* are *my priorities and am I truly living them out?*
- To avoid the activity trap:
  (1) Beware of the *subtle* expectations you may have for your children, the things that come naturally to you but may not come naturally to them;
  (2) Beware of telling yourself that you're encouraging activities for your child's benefit—they may be for your own benefit in the praise you receive from your peers;
  (3) Beware of early comparisons between your children and others;
  (4) Keep in mind that the best way to stimulate a youngster's brain is through multisensory stimulation, namely social and familial interaction at home.

Is Your Heart Turned Toward Home?

I suspect the following conversation is happening across America among parents who approach the decision to have children with all the emotional investment of joining their grocery store's buyer's reward program.

One night, after driving home their pair of cars from their pair of jobs to their gated-community house, two spouses look out over the clubhouse swimming pool at a pod of youngsters.

"Maybe we should have some of those . . . you know . . . what do you call them?"

"Children?"

"Yeah, children. Let's have a couple of those."

"Okay—but I'm not going to quit my job."

"Of course not. Nobody does that anymore."

They order their children and the package arrives by FedEx nine-month shipping. Their busy schedules continue, seemingly unruffled by this acquisition. They interview caregivers and spend truckloads of money entertaining their brand-new offspring, fresh out of the wrapping.

The dual-track binge continues, the couple trading cars and houses like baseball cards, taking regular vacations to Oahu and other places no one can spell.

Their lives go on, but no one connects.

When you have kids, your family's center of gravity should shift. I don't mean making your child the center of the universe. But whether you have one child or a baker's dozen, life is no longer just about the two of you. Mom may have to shift her workout routine to include curling that infant; Dad will have to give up babying his car and start babying the baby. Long, candlelit evenings at the local Italian restaurant may be replaced by drive-through visits to fast-food joints.

Life goes on when kids arrive, but it doesn't go on the same way. That's hard for many parents to grasp—perhaps harder than ever, thanks to the way our society has upshifted gears during the last 50 years.

Pressure Cooker

The 1950s was a decade of great optimism. Illustrations depicting the future—our present day—showed men and women lounging on the decks of anti-gravity homes and smiling as they boarded air buses. People believed technology would make life a breeze, freeing up more leisure time to spend together.

What happened? Today, rather than using technology to our advantage, we seem to let technology take advantage of us. Despite time-saving inventions, our pace of life has increased. A recent tongue-in-cheek article, "The Hurried Man,"[1] offered humorous advice on squeezing the most out of every second—including advice on how to eat faster, make up with your wife faster, and even die faster.

Time, once valued less than money, is now valued *more* than money. While people used to sacrifice time to save money, now they sacrifice money to save time. We pay top dollar for express mail, home grocery delivery service, and one-hour photo development.

As in everything, children are following our lead. One study found that time spent on homework more than doubled for six-to-eight-year-olds between 1981 and 1997.[2] At Toys R Us online, you can buy PDAs (personal digital assistants) for kids to schedule homework between soccer practice and Cub Scouts. The idea that an elementary school child would need this is frightening.

Children are stressed at every turn, inundated with material things and experiences. Teachers and youth pastors are finding kids burned out by their late teens.

How can this be, when we have more disposable time than ever? I'm convinced it's because we haven't gotten our priorities straight. As parents, we need to start by modeling a reasonable way of life—clearing our schedules to spend leisurely time with our families.

What Every Kid Wants

My love for fishing is almost innate. We have photos of me as a child wearing my father's knee boots as hip-waders. My mother, who recognized my passion early on, would walk me the quarter mile to Ellicott Creek almost every summer day until I grew old enough to go there myself with my little fishing pole and worms wriggling in my pocket.

Though Ellicott Creek gave me untold hours of pleasure, the one thing it didn't have was trout. Trout season, which opened in western New York on April 1, always held a mystique for me as a boy; I'd never caught a trout in my life. After every opening day, the local newspaper ran a photograph showing trout fishermen lined up elbow to elbow—

so many lines in the water they could have woven a net. I wanted to join them.

One year, the day after that picture appeared in the paper, I walked into a sporting goods store and for 60 cents bought a little plastic lure in the shape of a hellgrammite, a several-legged bug. I still recall asking my father if he would take me to that trout stream in the photo. It was probably 10-15 miles away as the crow flies, certainly more than a 9-year-old boy could walk.

My father had an eighth grade education, worked hard, and didn't have the leisure time parents have today. As a result, he almost never went fishing. I wanted so badly for him to go that day, but he couldn't— or wouldn't.

So I made the familiar trip down to Ellicott Creek myself and began fishing for trout, knowing full well that there weren't any there. I stood the entire day in a flooded creek so murky the trout wouldn't have been able to find the hook even if they'd miraculously showed up hungry.

My father, perhaps unwittingly, made a memory.

Your kid may come up to you with a request that seems silly, far-fetched, or just bothersome. Without even thinking about it, you may say, "Not now, honey," or "Maybe next week," or "Why don't you just go play on your Xbox?" You may never think about that request again.

But that doesn't mean your child will forget it.

I don't bear any ill will toward my father. I'm sure he forgot about my request less than three hours after I made it. He didn't realize he was making a memory, but I hope *you* do. Is that the kind of memory you want your kids to have of you?

I know, I know. You may think it's more important to wax your car or clean out the garage than to help junior patch together a cardboard rocket he's planning on flying to the moon. But behind those childish ways is a heart that wants little else than to spend time with *you*.

This is true even of adolescents. In the annual *State of our Nation's Youth* survey by the Horatio Alger Association, U.S. teens were asked where they'd most like to spend more time. Hanging out with their families was the top choice, chosen over visiting with friends, playing sports, working out, watching TV, or surfing the Web.[3]

Your kids aren't all that interested in your promotion to Vice President of Marketing. They aren't interested in how your presentation went in Chicago. They aren't interested in your bridge score or how much Mary Kay product you sold last quarter.

They *are* interested in whether you're at their ballgame when they hit their first line-drive single, or whether you're in the elementary school auditorium to hear them scratch out that violin solo you've endured at home for the last seven weeks. They care that you tell them their favorite story—the unabridged version—at bedtime over and over and over again, and that you see them manage to stay up on two wheels for more than twenty feet as they learn to ride the bicycle, and that you kiss their skinned elbows when they fall down.

Time together makes the difference.

I heard of a boy in a progressive school who was taking part in individualized education. One day he said, "Hey, can we have one of those days when we . . . um . . . when we used to . . . you know . . ." He stumbled as he searched for the right word. "Talk? That's it! Could we just *talk* again?"

Statistics show that most kids want exactly that—to "just talk again" with their parents. According to George Barna's survey results in his book *Real Teens*, "The most common substantive changes suggested [by teens regarding their relationship with their fathers] were the need to spend more time together (mentioned by 19 percent)," and "wanting better communication (13 percent)."[4]

Does that surprise you? If it does, let it sink in, because beneath their

PlayStation-playing, mp3-music-collecting, DVD-watching behavior, that's really what your kids want.

Under Your Influence

During the spring of 2000, Bill Cosby and I were asked to participate in a presentation to 10,000 people in Oklahoma City on preventing violence. I was Cosby's opening act, though I conned myself into thinking that they'd really come to see me!

Before the program, after we'd hammed it up for pictures and completed the handshaking, I spent a little over a half hour backstage alone with Cosby. He's a Temple Owl fan and I'm an Arizona Wildcats fan, so we hit it off by talking about basketball. After a while, our talk turned to the topic of the evening—the influence of families on today's youth.

Cosby, whose son had been violently murdered, wanted to know what I thought about what was happening to families in our society today. The answer we discussed backstage emerged time and again that evening in our interaction with the audience. Parents—not drugs, not movies, not peer groups—are a child's number one influence.

It came as no surprise to me. But in a culture in which we complain about all the influences on a child's life, it's important to remember that parents *are* what make the difference. Your words, your silence, your presence, your absence, your example—both good and bad—all matter more in the life of your child than you may ever realize.

Why am I so sure? Well, let me tell you a bit of my own life story.

There's No Place Like Home

At 19 years old, I packed my bags and left home. At the time I lived with my parents in Arizona, but I *hated* Arizona. A buddy back in New

York had told me I could live with him for a while, so I packed and headed across the country to his house, footloose and fancy-free. Unfortunately, my friend was good at drinking beer and lousy at following through on his word.

I arrived after dark in my 1950 Ford. My friend's parents were still awake, judging by the light inside. I didn't feel comfortable introducing myself and explaining I would be staying with them. I decided to wait; my buddy was supposed to meet me here at 11:30 P.M., after he finished work. Finally the lights winked off as his parents turned in for the night.

Eleven-thirty came and went. The temperature dropped, which would have been bearable except that my beloved Ford had no heater. The minutes sleepwalked slowly into morning as I sat shivering, freezing my Rumplestiltskin off.

That night I had plenty of time to think. When I closed my eyes and pulled my jacket around me, I imagined slipping under that comforter on my single bed in my parents' home, 2,500 miles away. I would have paid a lot of money to be in that place I'd taken for granted. I missed that priceless home court advantage.

Eventually I came to realize that my parents' undying love and support had made all the difference in my life. Finally it drew me back home.

Maybe that's why the song "I'll Be Home for Christmas" always makes me cry. It's a melancholy piece of music that reminds me of the simple gift of home and good times with my family growing up. It wasn't a perfect home—but it *was* a good home, and that's usually enough for most kids. Remember, we're not talking about the home court *heaven*. We're talking about the home court *advantage*.

Home is what you dream about when you're away, especially during holidays. Or when you're shivering in your car along a Buffalo side street, thousands of miles from that place you most want to be.

Homing Instincts

When our oldest kids were young, I used to drop them off at Grandma's to "pend" the night, as they called it then. They all loved going to Grandma's, but felt that homing instinct pulling them back to their own nest. By the time I got home from dropping them off, I could count on the phone ringing. I didn't need caller ID in those days to know who it was.

Krissy.

It was always Krissy, calling to talk about what they were doing and to chat with us. Of all our children, Krissy seemed to be most in tune with the advantages of being on her own home court. Her love of family continues today. She's what I call a "family-centered person," one whose homing instinct is strong.

Home ought to be a refuge, a place your children return to again and again because it's where they feel most secure. The word *parent* comes from the Latin word *parentis*, which means "protector." I'm speaking not only of physical protection, but also protection from conforming to the world's cookie-cutter selfishness. To do so, both you and your children have to spend plenty of time at home.

For example, I recommend celebrating significant events such as birthdays *in the home*. No, Ronald McDonald won't pass out goodies in your kitchen, and that Cheese-Breath Rodent won't serve your birthday boy his pizza if you don't visit his restaurant. But by making home the centerpiece of family life, you're creating positive memories for your kids in a place they can return to for the rest of their lives. A home court is a place that's familiar, that you've been to many times, that you know like the back of your hand and can call up by memory whenever you want to go back there, even if only in your mind. Such an advantage takes years to build—and the most important memories of your life to maintain.

To be a good parent, you don't have to be superhuman. As I often tell moms and dads, you can be a bird, you can be a plane—but whatever you do, don't be Super Parent! But if you want to be a good parent, home has to be the center of your heart.

So What'll It Be?

When those behind the counter of that Baskin Robbins of Life take your order, what'll it be? As much as you may want to pile on every flavor, you can only choose a few scoops before your cone becomes impossible to balance. True success is built on affirmation, relational involvement, and a sense of belonging—not on memorizing facts, intellectual stimulation, and never-ending activity.

Mel Brooks received a record 12 Tony awards for his Broadway play *The Producers.* When asked about the key to his success, he answered, "You know, my feet never touched the floor until I was two because they were always passing me around and kissing and hugging me."[5]

How will your kids describe your home when they grow up? Will they remember a dad who had a lucrative career and a low golf handicap, but who rarely spent significant time at home? If so, how will you feel when your grown son becomes a CEO and isn't much interested in his own kids, let alone spending time with you?

Most of us will readily admit that nothing in life—no *thing*—compares in importance to relationships. So why trade family for a boat, or seats on committees, or even the adulation of other church members for being "so involved"?

Maybe accomplishments, material possessions, or career positions seem crucial now. I promise you, though, that when you near the end of your life, you'll know that relationships matter most.

Why not recognize that truth today, while you still have time to do something about it?

Let's Remember:

- When you have kids, your family should adjust accordingly; you can't continue your same routine.
- Technology doesn't necessarily simplify things; evaluate how much time gadgets give to or take from your life.
- Ask yourself: *Who has really made a difference in my life—and why? What kind of memories do I want my kids to have of me?*
- "Hanging out with their families" was the top choice given by U.S. teens for where they would most like to spend more time.
- Everyone wants her child to succeed, but not everyone defines success. True success is built on affirmation, relational involvement, and a sense of belonging—not on memorizing facts, intellectual stimulation, and never-ending activity.

"Busy Children Are Happy Children"

And Other Modern Myths

uiz time!

Which of the following statements are true, and which are false?

- It's not the quantity of time with my kids that matters, it's quality that counts.
- I'm a good parent if I make many sacrifices for my child.
- Children should be free to express themselves any way they want.
- My child deserves the things I didn't have growing up, the things most kids today have.
- A full plate of activities is good for kids—let them absorb all they can.
- A gifted child is a successful child.
- Starting my child early in school gives him an extra edge.

- It's important that my child finish first.
- If my child sets his mind to it, he can do anything.

Did you find yourself answering *true* to any of these questions? If so, you've fallen for some of today's more popular parenting myths. Even if you caught on and answered *false* to every one, you may have thought, *Now, what's wrong with* that, *Dr. Leman?*

Let's look at some of the myths that lure us into the activity trap— and away from raising homegrown kids who enjoy the home court advantage.

Myth 1: It's Not the Quantity of Time That Matters, It's the Quality That Counts

"Great news!" a husband calls to his wife as he heads out the front door with his golf clubs slung over his shoulder. "The Smiths have agreed to videotape Clovis's piano recital while I'm on the course with the new client. I honestly didn't know how I'd pull it off, but somehow I managed. I'll be back this evening to tuck in Clovis!"

Trust me—when nervous little Clovis looks into the audience before his recital and sees the reflecting glass of the video camera lens instead of his father's caring eyes, it's not going to be much of a consolation. Especially if Dad already told Clovis he'd be there.

"But it was just *like* being there!" Dad might argue. "I made sure Mr. Smith caught everything on tape!"

What Dad doesn't realize is that while *he* may have felt he was there, his absence felt like a huge black hole for Clovis. It was a screaming statement of noninterest and poor priorities.

Oh, yeah. Dad shouldn't be surprised if, when he tries to tuck little Clovis in tonight, the boy pretends to be already asleep.

You can't cheat a child in your priorities and then somehow make it up with a bit of "quality time"—which is almost always defined by the parent's convenience and availability, not the kid's preference. Even children who can't divide 10 by 2 can be razor sharp when it comes to the mathematics of priority. Even if you *are* able to fool them for a little while with trinkets brought back from business trips, eventually they'll figure out what those "souvenirs" cost them: time with you.

A toddler doesn't think abstractly. She sees that you're around or you aren't. Whether you're away at work, on the golf course, or volunteering at your church doesn't really make much difference. All she registers in that little brain of hers is that you're there or not. And yes, she is asking the question, "If he really does love me like he says, why doesn't he want to spend more time with me?"

Generally speaking, the more your child sees her parents, the more stability and less uncertainty there is in her life. This doesn't mean you should make her the center of the universe, but your regular physical and emotional presence, even in small ways, makes a big difference.

This may make you feel guilty—or you can see it as an opportunity. Imagine the impact you can have by taking your young son or daughter out to lunch every other week or so. Or instead of sitting in your favorite chair with your face behind the newspaper, why not read it with your child at the table and discuss it? My daughter Holly and I read *USA Today* together every morning for years; I reached for the sports section and she got the entertainment section. She still talks about those times with great fondness.

When I was growing up, my father scratched my back while we watched TV together. Halfway through a 30-minute program we'd switch and I'd scratch his back. I value the memory of those times more than I do any car I've owned or any house I've bought. Even kids who didn't get enough of their parents, or who came from troubled homes, cherish the few good moments they did have.

Why do we so readily accept the myth of quality time over quantity time? Because doing so helps us rationalize our selfish behaviors. We're committed to chasing our own rainbows—maintaining a perfect home, following every sports event aired on ESPN (while watching ESPN2 and ESPN Classic during the commercials), even garnering peer approval for our involvement in church activities. And we're not about to let our kids get in the way!

For a child, the *quantity* of time you spend together is part of what makes it a *quality* experience. If after dinner tonight you were to set before your three-year-old child a very small, single scoop of Godiva Belgian dark chocolate ice cream in one bowl and a large mixing bowl heaped high with your local supermarket's freezer-burned brand in the other, which would he choose? The bowlful, of course. For kids, quantity matters. That's why a kid can smell his way blindfolded to any all-you-can-eat pizza place in town.

Yes, quantity time should be quality time, too—more than simply logging minutes in the parent/child flight book. But *more* is part of the equation that makes that time *better.* Traveling sports teams and after-school clubs may be stimulating and educational, but signing your child up for even three of these activities simultaneously cuts quantity *and* quality. The *advantage* comes from being at *home,* and you can't do that on the road.

Myth 2: I'm a Good Parent If I Make Many Sacrifices for My Child

I was on the phone with one seven-year-old's parents. They'd given their son the world. Unfortunately, he was relishing the role of tyrannical little Julius Caesar.

At first glance, you might be surprised. This was a tightly knit family with a strong faith, and the parents wanted nothing more than for their son to succeed. In fact, his success was the basket into which they'd piled all their eggs. They'd given him every opportunity on the face of the earth and even prepared him for one or two beyond—space camp, for example, when he was only four years old.

They couldn't understand why their son, rather than assuming the ambition of that future astronaut, was hatching into a little alien. He was well behaved in school, but didn't finish any work. At home he was beginning to mouth off at Mom and Dad.

As I talked with them it quickly became evident that the problem wasn't that they'd been uninvolved in his life. They'd *overdone* it.

Fully half the parents who've walked through my counseling door have overparented—either due to perfectionist expectations or simply by revolving around the child as if he were the center of the family's universe.

Overparent? you may think. *How can you overdo it on love?*

When you overparent, you weaken the child's self-image, suffocating him so that he or she may come to believe, *I guess I don't have what it takes to get by without Dad's and Mom's help. They obviously don't believe I can finish anything by myself, so it's probably better to not complete things. Then they can't criticize my unfinished project and me.* The child may not say or even consciously think that, but it's what's going on.

Some parents think they're sacrificing when they overparent. What they're really doing, though, is hovering.

Imagine a hovering boss with impossibly high standards. After a few months of working for him, you'd sink into your chair at seeing that shadow across your shoulder. You'd dread new projects, and start dreaming of jobs in more relaxing fields—point man on the bomb squad, air traffic controller at the world's busiest airport. Is that really how you want your kids to look at you, dreading that "Tsk, tsk" as you look over their shoulders or jumping when you enter the room?

A hover-boss's attitude says, *You will fail without my constant supervision.* The "sacrificing" perfectionist parent sends the same message.

A homegrown parent is not the same as a hovering parent. Being at home with your kids doesn't mean you have to be their quality control inspector or entertainer. My youngest daughter, Lauren, went through a stage when she was six in which she complained about being bored as soon as she was by herself. Five minutes after playing with a friend or older sibling, she'd trudge up to me with the longest of long faces and complain, "I'm soooo booooorrrrred."

I didn't "sacrifice" by jumping up and pulling out a Monopoly game or sprinting to the cupboard to get some paper, scissors, and glue. I just smiled and said, "Honey, you can be bored all day long if you want. When you're finished being bored, welcome back to life; it's great!" I'm not the recreational director of the Leman family. If kids want to be bored, so be it!

Hovering can happen so innocently. Little Buford, having stubbed his toe, may be hanging on to Mommy's leg to get her attention; Mommy picks Buford up, comforts him, and perhaps overdoes it a bit in the process. Next time Buford gets hurt, he'll expect the same emergency room care—complete with the Popsicle to make him feel better!

Overdo it enough, and you'll reinforce habits you don't want to instill. And you don't want to create habits that last into your child's graduate school education.

When does helping become hurting? In general, parents shouldn't do things that the kid can do for himself.

This doesn't mean I won't pour milk on Lauren's cereal in the morning, even though she can do it herself with minimal splashing. She loves it when I handle the big gallon of milk, and I don't mind doing that. It's an expression of caring and nurtures our relationship.

But let's say Lauren has decided she's not going to follow through on a commitment. She wants me to make a phone call for her, announcing that she's backing out. In that instance I'd say, "*You* call Mrs. Johnson and tell her that you're unable to babysit. You're the one who told her you would. You call and tell her you can't."

Making that call on her behalf might feel like love, but it would only stunt her growth. The "sacrifice" wouldn't do either of us any good.

Don't do your kid's dirty work. If your child consistently leaves projects undone or approaches tasks with all the enthusiasm of an anesthetized sloth, he or she may be under the shadow of a hovering parent.

As for that father and mother with the junior Julius Caesar, I told them to exercise the courage to be imperfect parents—doctor's orders. They were simply trying too hard to do everything. Their boy was bright, but would waste his academic years if they didn't back off and let him repeat second grade.

Often the best sacrifice you can make for your child is that of your own subtle expectations.

Myth 3: Children Should Be Free to Express Themselves Any Way They Want

Sande and I were in a restaurant with a woman we hadn't seen in years—and her two little boys. Her sons were cuter than cute, the kind you'd find on a breakfast cereal commercial or Saturday morning kids' show. But like stereotypical child stars, they were unmanageable.

One of them, a four-year-old, was clearly trained in sibling torture techniques. He began digging his fingernails into my leg under the table. Perhaps it was my contorted face that caused Mommy to try to divert his attention. In response, he started hitting her.

"Oh, that's boys for you!" the woman said as she tickled him to make light of it.

Lady, I thought, *boys* are *different from girls.* But boys and girls alike need discipline; at times they need lines drawn in the sand to know they can't hit, hold their sisters hostage, or stage a minivan mutiny.

I'm all for nurturing kids' personalities and gifts. But anyone who believes that children are born with angel wings should toss a candy bar into the "Duck, Duck, Goose" circle to see the little devils come out. Boundaries have to be drawn. We don't want to encourage *all* that children are.

My good friend Dr. James Dobson tells the story of the school that tore down its playground fences so kids wouldn't feel confined. Instead of playing right up to where the fences had been, however, children clustered in the center of the open space. Kids draw strength, stability, and esteem from boundaries, and need them to define what is safe and what isn't.

Many parents today want their kids to be whoever they are without any constraints. But you deny your parental wisdom when you let your child take the reins.

You don't have to relinquish your responsibility to the "experts," the media, or teachers—let alone your own children. Homegrown kids have boundaries.

Myth 4: My Child Deserves the Things I Didn't Have Growing Up, the Things Most Kids Today Have

Let me put this up-front so you can't miss it: the home court advantage is not about giving your kids the best equipment; it's about giving them love, care, and security.

Recently our daughter Lauren tried out for the school softball team.

We thought it was great, but we didn't jump in and drop $500 on the latest equipment. She used her older sister's mitt, and since there was already enough aluminum to build an entire house leaning against the dugout walls, we figured she didn't need to own a bat. There were plenty to borrow.

Soon after practices started, she opened up a dinner conversation by saying, "Dad, I need to get spikes."

Notice: Not "*May* I have spikes," but "I *need* to get spikes."

"Oh really?" I said. "You know, honey, I played ball for a long time—even made the all-star team—and I didn't have spikes."

"But everybody else has them!" Lauren said.

"Well, we'll see," I said.

I purposely didn't give her a definite answer. Instead, I went to her practices and saw that while some of the kids did have cleats, quite a few didn't. As the first game grew closer, though, all the girls except Lauren got baseball shoes. Some looked so geared-up you'd think they were playing for the Arizona Diamondbacks.

I still didn't buy Lauren cleats. I'm well aware of what that does to a 70-pound kid; it could create a hundred pounds of peer pressure. I agreed with Lauren that everybody else had baseball shoes. "But I don't want you to be like everybody else," I explained.

I didn't say this to her, but if Lauren is like "everybody else," there's a very high probability she'll experiment with drugs and lose her virginity before she gets her high school diploma. Being like everybody else is about the *worst* argument she could feed me!

Money wasn't the main issue. *So if you can afford it,* you may ask, *why not?*

Here's why: I don't want my child to expect that when she joins the hobby-of-the-month club, I'll fully outfit her with the latest hi-tech gear. Young kids change their interests more frequently than their underwear; if you buy all the equipment every time, you'll soon be opening a used sporting goods store in your garage. And your child will learn that whenever she wants something, all she has to do is turn to Dad or Mom to meet her every desire.

If you want homegrown kids, what kind of indelible imprint do you want to leave on them? Do what every other parent does, and you're saying it's best to go along with the crowd, just do what everybody else does—whether or not doing so makes sense.

I want to wait a year to see whether Lauren is going to stick with softball. If she does, I might even shell out a few bucks and buy her a new mitt as well as some baseball shoes—but don't count on it.

You may think I'm an ogre for allowing my daughter to play softball in tennis shoes. You may think she feels deprived. But her face will light up when she tells you about coming home and saying, "Dad, you gotta pitch to me and throw me some fly balls," and I'll get out my ridiculously old mitt, which she'll laugh at, and we'll have a good time creating memories lasting a hundred times longer than a size 6 pair of spikes.

Shelling out $60 for a pair of shoes doesn't require much commitment or sacrifice. Being home before Lauren, and being free to practice with her—that asks a bit more. That's a *real* advantage.

You know what's interesting? Lauren forgot about the shoes. Once her teammates got used to seeing her in tennis shoes, it was no big deal.

What we give our kids doesn't mean that much. What does matter? Our commitment. Our presence. Our input. Lauren knows I won't pay $60 for her shoes, but she also knows I'd lay down my life for her. If she needed a kidney transplant, I'd be first in line even if it was my last one. Blood transfusion? Drain me dry if that's what it takes.

I'm amazed at how many parents don't have a realistic concept of what constitutes excess. I believe that misconception comes from the idea that if we love our children we'll give them everything they want that we can afford. We fear that if we don't give them what others have, they'll resent us or fall behind. I'm more interested in cultivating realistic expectations and a thankful heart.

For example, when Hannah turned 16, we still had a steam-powered computer that she used to do her homework and e-mail friends. It was slower than molasses running uphill, and it had less memory than a two-day-old baby.

"Dad," my son, Kevin, said, "in two years Hannah's heading off to college and she'll need a computer. The one we have now is so old it won't run any of the new programs she's going to need. Why don't you consider getting her a notebook computer? An Apple iBook would be a great choice."

Sande and I know more about quantum physics and ancient Aramaic than we do about computers—which is to say, nothing at all. To me, a "hard drive" is a difficult commute home, and I wouldn't think of "burning a CD" without a permit from the fire department. But Kevin knows his stuff.

Hannah was thrilled. She got a computer without even asking for it! Not once did she ever say with an attitude, "I want a computer!"

"Did you see the note?" Sande asked me the morning after we'd given Hannah her computer. I walked into the kitchen and there was a note on a paper plate:

I just want to thank you again. I love you guys so much; thank you for my computer.
                                        —Your Hannah

Your Hannah.

That's a phrase every homegrown parent shoots for. It's the kind of thing worth writing—or e-mailing—home about.

Now if only I could figure out how to work the computer's flimsy cup holder that slides out the side . . .

Myth 5: A Full Plate of Activities Is Good for Kids— Let Them Absorb All They Can

"As captain of the junior varsity volleyball team, first-chair flute in the school orchestra, a top player on the tennis team and an honors student with three hours of homework a night, Andrea Galambos, who was also taking singing and art classes after school, put in 18-hour days. 'I never had more than five minutes to sit down and breathe,' says Andrea, 16, a junior at Staples High School in Westport, Connecticut. Some mornings she didn't want to get out of bed because of all the stuff she had to do."[1]

I couldn't make up a worse recipe for a balanced and fulfilling home life if I tried.

Many kids' activity schedules rival an Olympiad's training routine. Some parents take perverse pride in this overcommitment because they're running the rat race themselves and wear their busyness like a medal. Unfortunately, they end up pulling their kids along.

But Dr. Leman, you might say, *you keep talking about overcommitment but you're not specific. How much is too much?*

You really want to know? I recommend only one activity per child per term. When Lauren wanted to be in Brownies, that's what she did. When she's in softball, that's her activity.

Too many parents have been duped into thinking that busy hands are happy hands. Those hands may be happy for a while; kids may enjoy, even choose, gymnastics class over a family picnic. But even though activities may entertain us, exercise our bodies and minds, and teach us valuable lessons, they don't bond us as a family unless we're doing them together.

If your adolescent daughter practices softball every night and travels every weekend to tournaments across the state, the odds are slim that you'll be with her when she needs a shoulder to cry on about the breakup with her boyfriend. You can't have regular, meaningful conversation if your kids are always out of the house learning how to hit a low-hanging curve ball or return a backhand volley.

Unscheduled free time together around your house opens relational opportunities you otherwise wouldn't have. Activities can be good in moderation, but time with family at home produces home-grown kids.

Rejecting the Myths

Just as we need to reject the myths of "free love," the "benefits" of living together before marriage, and the mistake of no-fault divorce, we must carefully avoid the misconceptions of child-rearing. We haven't dealt with all of them yet; we'll cover the rest in the next chapter.

Let's Remember:

- In addition to the quality of time you spend with your children, the quantity also matters to them.
- Parents of homegrown children don't make their children the center of the universe, hovering over them and sacrificing everything for them.
- Children should not be free to do everything they please; they need boundaries.

- Your child doesn't necessarily need the things you didn't have growing up, the things most kids today seem to have.
- Give children what they need, not what they want.
- An endless supply of outside activities isn't good for kids; free time at home is better.

4

"If He Sets His Mind to It, My Child Can Do Anything"

And Other Modern Myths II

I n the last chapter we looked at a few mistaken ideas that can keep us from raising homegrown kids. Let's put a few more of these myths under the microscope.

Myth 6: "A Gifted Child Is a Successful Child"

Occasionally, following one of my talks, a parent will introduce himself or herself and begin with a familiar statement: "My child is gifted."

The parent's tone seems to imply that heaven is focusing all its attention on this truly extraordinary soul, and the rest of the world should get out of the way and pay homage. It's just a matter of time until this "gifted" child gets a recording or publishing or sports contract, or a lucrative job offer from a Fortune 500 company.

"Oh, I'm so sorry," I like to reply. "My condolences."

Inevitably, the parent stands there blinking. "W-what do you mean?" he or she stammers, stunned that anyone would treat this news with anything but enthusiasm.

That's understandable. Most people believe a "success" is one who's risen to the top and contributes to society. And what child is better positioned for this ascent than the gifted one, a regular little monkey when it comes to scrambling up the proverbial "ladder of success"?

The truth is that we're all on a horizontal axis together; not one of us is "better" than the next guy. I don't look down at my kids from a patriarchal top rung, for example. We need each other because we're journeying through life together. Therein lies the strength of family.

Life has a way of putting not only our gifts to the test, but, more importantly, our character—who we are. Whether or not your child has a cornucopia of talents, it's how he or she uses them that matters.

"It's not what you do, it's who you are," I tell my kids. Gifts are tools; they're only as good as the one who wields them. Your son may be able to recite the value for *pi* to the tenth digit, but how fairly does he divide his candy with his siblings? Your daughter may be a cheerleader, homecoming queen, and valedictorian—but how well does she treat the "anonymous" girls who walk invisibly down the halls at school?

Intellect is a wonderful thing—but being smart can get your child in jail as easily as it can get him into M.I.T. (ever hear of insider trading or computer hacking?). Gifts without character are like a Formula One race car without much rubber left on the tires—fast in the straightaways, but dangerous in the turns. Life is mostly about navigating those turns, some of them hairpin sharp.

Whether your child is gifted or not, help prepare him for life by focusing on his attitude rather than his accomplishments. That requires plenty of interaction at home, rather than always watching him excel on the stage or the basketball court.

Myth 7: "Starting My Child Early in School Gives Him an Extra Edge"

Is your child a "little bluebird"?

Little bluebirds know their colors and can sing their way through the alphabet. They can count from 1 to 10 in Spanish along with their favorite *Sesame Street* characters, and flit from word to word in their favorite book. And if that little bluebird has a fall birthday, academically it may seem to make sense to start him in school a year early.

Please don't.

The advantage, remember, is on the *home* court.

If academics are the primary basis for starting your child early, you're probably doing him or her a disservice. Socially and emotionally your child may not be ready. When faced with the choice of making a child the youngest or oldest kindergartener, I'll opt for the oldest 9 times out of 10 (there are exceptions to this that we'll address in Chapter 9).

This decision won't always make a difference right away. It may not pay off until the curriculum changes significantly—in fourth grade, for example—or when the child's body starts changing in middle school. Not starting a kid early can make a tremendously positive difference in his life, especially for boys.

Puberty is that time when girls may twitter about marrying the male P.E. teacher, while boys still relate to the female English teacher as if she's their mother. We've known for over half a century that girls mature more quickly than boys. Giving your son that extra year for his body to grow can be a potent confidence builder when he hits the teen years, especially if he has any interest in athletics.

Notice I said "confidence builder," not "give him a better shot at making starting quarterback in the Rose Bowl." The emotional and social aspects of your child's development are much more important than whether he's first or second string *anything*. Rather than rushing him into Urchin University at age three, keep him at home to love and play with him. When school comes along, great; learning is important.

If you're still considering starting your child in school a year early or having her skip a grade, ask yourself these questions:

- Is this a decision I'm making for myself or for my child?
- Will this further crowd an already busy family social calendar?
- Is this decision being made to allow Mom or Dad to return to work a year earlier?
- Is it primarily for financial reasons?
- Is it to keep up with a sibling, neighbor, relative, or best friend's son or daughter?

If you answered yes to any of the above, please reconsider. The only thanks you receive may be the confidence you see in your child a decade down the road. But if your focus is your child's welfare and not "keeping up with the Joneses," what more encouragement do you need?

Let your homegrown children be children; don't hurry them.

Myth 8: "It's Important That My Child Finish First"

When I was 12, I got to join the local All-Star Little League team. I played third base—the "hot corner." The problem was, I wasn't so hot.

Nevertheless, I felt as if I were in heaven as our team played All-Star teams from other towns. But one game was not a heavenly experience. In the bottom of the last inning, we were up by one run with one out to go. With runners for their team on both second and third, our coach decided to move a few players around; I switched from third base to first.

The final batter hit a grounder to my replacement at third base. As their tying run crossed home plate and their game-winning run was rounding third, the third baseman fielded the ball and fired it to me. All I had to do was catch it and the game would be over.

I dropped the ball.

Their winning run crossed the plate. Our team lost—or, more accurately, I lost the game for us.

The other team went wild as our team stood in stunned disbelief.

I quietly began to cry.

I still remember the words echoing in my head: *Hey, stupid, all you had to do to win the game was catch the ball!*

That's a vivid memory. But what the coach did next stands out even more vividly.

As our team slowly filed back to the third base side where our dugout was, he walked to where I stood at first. He put his arm around me and walked with me back across the field.

"Cub," he said, using my nickname at the time, "without you we wouldn't have gotten this far."

Those words, and his arm around me, made all the difference in the world. He could have shattered me emotionally. Instead, he gave me the rare gift of confidence and perspective.

Most of us discover early that we don't always finish first. One of the most important lessons a child can learn is how to finish *last,* how to experience and learn from failure time after time—because life is filled with it.

Unfortunately, many parents feel their primary responsibility is to test the limits of their child's ability, to see whether he or she might be the next Michael Jordan or Mary Lou Retton. But it's much more important to prepare our kids to live with their limitations than to give them an expectation of unbroken success.

Game-winning grand slams are not what make us who we are. What makes you who you are is how you get back into the batter's box of life after you strike out. Not having your own way or finishing atop the dog pile of life is not the worst thing in the world. It can be training in humility—the kind of thing your homegrown kid may need someday when he's married and has to know how to put his spouse's feelings first.

Myth 9: "If My Child Sets His Mind to It, He Can Do Anything"

If you set your mind to it, you can accomplish a lot—that's true. But no matter how hard I try, you won't see my sixty-year-old self leading the four-man bobsled team at the next Winter Olympics. You *can't* do anything just because you set your mind to it.

Sounds obvious, doesn't it? But the implications extend further than many of us want to admit. For example, lots of kids love to sing and imagine themselves bopping around on stage. Yet only a few will have the voice and opportunity to succeed professionally. In fact, those who sing like me won't have a chance of making it in the church choir, much less at Madison Square Garden.

Does that mean your daughter won't *enjoy* singing? Hardly. Does that mean you shouldn't affirm her desire to sing in the school choir, and instead put her in something where she can be the best? Absolutely not. But it does mean she probably won't win the next *American Idol* competition, or cut a platinum album. (Though having heard some of today's music, I will make exceptions to this.) If you have your mind fixed on that dream, you're setting yourself—and her—up for frustration.

A good coach with a healthy perspective on life can tell whether your child has enough natural talent to go far in a given sport. Mark McGwire's dad kept him out of organized baseball until he was 12—and then Mark hit a home run his first time at bat! Most true sports prodigies—the kind that can actually make a living at their game—show their talent early. Even if your kid is the best player in Peoria, he'll literally have to compete with the world to play professionally. Be realistic and emphasize character over skill.

Look for coaches who share this view. Some mentors' hyper-enthusiasm needs to be tempered with reality, especially if they're trying to live out their own dreams through their trainees. That's the very thing you're trying to avoid as the parent of a homegrown child!

When it comes to academics, some children simply aren't capable of being straight-A students no matter how hard they try. Yet many parents demand top grades for C students because without them their child can't get into the most prestigious colleges.

These parents worry all the time about their child's performance. They see those grades not only as a reflection of their child's worth, but their own. The fact is that grades are simply a measure of what a student has been able to achieve in the classroom. They may not even indicate whether he or she is learning.

Some of the best minds in history didn't do well in school. The school administration thought Albert Einstein was a brick short of a full load. Can you imagine little Albert's teacher looking over his shoulder?

"Albert, Albert, what are you doing? You're supposed to be practicing your *A*s and *B*s. What is that *E*, and that little *m* and *c*? And why are you using numbers? Albert, I will be calling your mother this afternoon!"

Your IQ has little to do with whether or not you're going to make a difference in the world as God sees it. Love is the greatest measure.

Not every kid will be the brightest bulb on the tree. Here are more vital issues for "homegrowing" parents:

- Did your child try hard?
- Did she learn perseverance and the value of work?
- Is she learning how to think, and how to be creative with the gifts she's been given?
- Is he a thoughtful friend in school?

The answers to those questions are more important than any column of A's on your child's report card.

Let's Remember:

- A gifted child is not necessarily a successful child.
- Don't rush your child to grow up. If there's a question on whether to start your child in kindergarten, hold him or her back. That extra year can make a world of difference in your child's confidence.
- In today's competitive world, it's important that your child learn to finish last—to fail with grace.
- No matter how hard your child tries, he will never be able to reach certain goals. A good parent recognizes a child's limitations.

5

Your Money or Your Life

How Spending Time and Treasure

Is Affecting the Home

Before the first television set arrived in our little western New York town back in the 1940s, radio was king. One of the most popular programs of the time was Jack Benny's comedy show. On March 28, 1948, the star aired one of his most humorous—and famous—skits ever. In that episode Benny's tightwad character was mugged while coming home.

"Don't make a move," the robber demanded. "This is a stickup."

"Wha—?"

"You heard me!"

"Mister . . . mister, put down that gun!"

"Shut up! Now, come on. Your money or your life!"

It only took a second or two before the studio audience, recognizing the dilemma for Benny's skinflint character, began laughing.

Exasperated, the robber yelled, "Look, bud, I said your *money* or your *life!*"

"I'm thinking it over!" Benny shot back.

The laugh that followed from the studio audience went on for two and a half minutes, the longest in radio history.

Funny as this is, Benny's response captures the sad truth of how many of us act when confronted with the choice between our *money*—our houses, cars, vacations—and our *lives*—our health, relationships with spouse and kids, and emotional and spiritual well-being. Like Benny's character, many of us can't seem to let go of our money, our overly demanding jobs, or our lavish lifestyles—even when the cost may be our families.

Have you examined the half-hour blocks in your Day-Timer and the entries in your checkbook register? That's where you'll find your priorities. When faced with the choice between your money or your life, you too may be standing there, shouting, "I'm thinking it over!"

Designer Babies

Madonna has one. So do Sarah Jessica Parker, Celine Dion, swimsuit model Elle MacPherson, and Gwyneth Paltrow.

"It" is a Silver Kensington Pram (fancy name for a baby stroller) that retails for a mere $2,200.

My first car cost a tenth of that!

You can accessorize that pram with a stylish Louis Vuitton diaper bag that sells for $1,070, or a Prada version that retails for a more modest $820.

Don't the parents shelling out these bucks realize what goes *in* a diaper bag?

When David Letterman finally became a dad, Madonna sent the

baby a pair of Little E.D.A. shearling baby booties. These hand-sewn sheepskin booties better keep those tootsies nice and toasty, though, since they set a person back $158—for a pair of shoes a baby probably will outgrow in two months.

If you *really* want to splurge, though, you can do what actor Chris O'Donnell did when he shelled out $4,599 for a two-story Bungalow playhouse. Basketball star Jason Kidd outdid that: He and his wife bought a Firehouse ($5,699) and a Cotton Candy Manor ($8,299).[1] That playhouse costs more than the home I grew up in!

Generally speaking, families in our culture are more affluent than ever. I realize you probably can gaze up that economic ladder and see at least a few people standing on a higher rung than yours. But if you aren't cooking your 87th variation on rice and beans, and have a solid roof over your head and decent clothes on your back, you're part of the upper crust of human history in terms of wealth.

Our kids, of course, seldom appreciate this truth.

"Dad," my daughter Lauren asked me one afternoon when I picked her up from school, "could we stop by Burger King?"

"Sure," I said. We made the detour and picked up a double cheeseburger, fries, and a cherry Slushie.

"You know, Lauren," I said as we pulled out of the parking lot, "as a child, I would never have *imagined* my father picking me up from school, because we walked to school."

"I know," she said between bites of cheeseburger. "Two miles."

"Exactly!" I said. "Two miles."

"And in the snow, Dad," she added.

"That's right! In the snow!"

Lauren may be tired of hearing the story, but that after-school trip truly would have been inconceivable to me when I was growing up. Like many families of the time, mine was poor; I remember cutting hot dogs in two to stretch the meal. My idea of high living was going to a Friday night high school basketball game with my parents, then heading to a restaurant called the Colonial House for a 30-cent hamburger and a 20-cent hot fudge sundae.

There's an advantage to growing up without everything your heart desires. You appreciate the little things.

Today, the world is a different place. Too many of us measure our worth by the year and model of our cars, the square footage and location of our houses, the brand labels on our children's clothes. Even the hours we put into our jobs and activities serve as a gauge of success.

The problem isn't money exactly. We need food, shelter, and clothing to survive. In most of our communities it's difficult to get by without owning a car, and it's nice to occasionally enjoy a few of the comforts of contemporary culture. The problem is our appetite for possessions and the lengths to which we'll go to "better" our lifestyles—often at the expense of time spent with our families.

You Get What You Pay For

When our first daughter, Holly, was 18 months old, Sande and I went shopping for a pair of patent leather shoes to complement her beautiful red dress and white stockings. When the salesman found exactly what we needed, it was time to ask that question stirring deep within me, that concern encoded into male DNA: "How much are they?"

"Thirty-two dollars," replied the salesperson.

Thirty-two dollars sounded like a great price for a TV back in 1974, but not for a pair of shoes. They weren't, after all, ruby slippers. At that point the shoes came flying off Holly faster than you could click your heels together and say, "There's no place like home."

I suppose we could have stretched our budget, bought the shoes, and worked a bit harder to pay them off. But spending more time at the office to afford patent leather shoes—or a more luxurious car or house, for that matter—isn't what we valued then, and it isn't what we value now.

The truth is, there *is* no place like home. Given the choice between patent leather shoes and more leisurely time together at home with the little girl trying them on, I'll choose time together any day.

Those shoes are simply one small example of how every decision we make comes with a price tag. The financial bottom line is only the beginning, and often isn't even the most costly. If you trade homegrown kids for store-bought goods, you'll get what you pay for—which may include a family living on leftover scraps of your time and energy.

Time Flies When You're Having Fun

When you drop $1,200 on the sporting goods store counter for a new set of golf clubs, that may seem like a great deal. But you aren't simply dropping hundreds of dollars from your recreation budget. You're declaring your intention to spend time swinging those clubs with friends, work colleagues, and clients. You're buying into Thursday evenings at the driving range and Friday mornings and Saturday afternoons on the back nine.

What's the real cost? Perhaps $1,200 plus 200 hours per year—which equals who-knows-how-many missed opportunities as your children grow up.

Eighteen years may seem like an eternity. But if your child is six years old, you're already one-third of the way through the time you have to raise him or her. If she's nine, half your days together have passed. Time really does fly when you're out having fun; if you aren't careful, those years when your child most wants to spend time with you will fly by faster than a golf ball careening off a titanium driver.

I know a young middle school assistant principal who takes this challenge seriously. Now nearing 40, he's decided he wants to run marathons. (Why anybody would want to do anything quite so stupid as run 26 miles without stopping is beyond me; if I want pain like that, I'll just hand you a two-by-four and tell you to whack me in the head.) Since training for a marathon requires many hours and his kids are young, I asked him, "When do you do the long runs?"

"It's kind of embarrassing," he answered.

"Go on—tell me."

"I wake up at 3:20 A.M. and run before work."

"So it's dark out the entire time you're running?"

"Yeah. I have a headlight. You see, there's no way I can come home from work at 5:00 P.M. and tell my kids, 'Sorry, but Daddy has to leave for another hour and a half.' If I want to run, I have to do it before work."

"When do you sleep?"

"I go to bed when my kids do. It might seem kind of silly, a grown man going to bed at 9 P.M., but that's what works best for my family."

It's not silly at all. The homegrown attitude bends his hobby around his family, rather than attempting to bend his family around his hobby. It's all about looking at the real cost. Hunting or fishing or hiking or whatever may provide enjoyment for you and your friends. But make sure those hours are balanced with plenty of time with your spouse and children.

Maybe you're more materially minded than activity-prone. You need to be just as careful. Know that new house with the bigger yard you just "have" to have? Ever thought about the time required to clean those extra rooms and landscape that yard? Yeah, you can hire a cleaning lady or a landscaper, but then you'll have another two regular, monthly expenses requiring you to bring in even more income.

The same principle applies when you purchase that new car on credit. I've heard of families with an annual income of $50,000 buying a new minivan for $25,000. They don't have the cash up-front, so after they make the interest payments (at least another $10,000), cover the tax and licenses and all that stuff, they've spent almost an entire year's income to buy one vehicle! Do you really want to spend 8 hours a day, 5 days a week, away from your family for 9 or 10 months so that you can buy a brand-new vehicle? Is that *really* a good trade?

There's no law that says you need a new minivan just because other families are getting them. Those other families may be growing apart as Mommy and Daddy fight because of the pressure over paying the bills.

Part of raising a homegrown family means purchasing wisely; otherwise, you'll have to leave home to dig yourself out of debt.

Bucks to Burn? Don't Burn Your Family

Remember that saying from the 1980s: "The one who finishes with the most toys wins"?

Wins what? More toys to pile on one's grave?

Not many people ask from their deathbed, "Would everyone please excuse us for a moment? I want a few minutes alone with my jewelry." No one asks to hold that set of golf clubs one last time, or for one final glimpse at their waxed and polished Lexus. Material possessions don't hold bedside vigils when your end is near; they can't cry with you in your pain, or laugh at shared stories.

I mention this because families with "bucks to burn" may be at a higher risk of misplacing priorities simply because they can afford it. When you have significant discretionary income, the blessed seeds of that situation can grow into cursed weeds. The Bible talks about the love of money as "a root of all kinds of evil."[2] It doesn't say that money *is* evil, but rather that it's a hothouse for trouble.

The temptations seem harmless enough. You may have the means for your child to pursue any activity that suits your fancy, from preschool French tutorials to gymnastics class three times a week to Suzuki violin lessons with a master teacher for your 18-month-old. But don't burn yourself and your family by thinking you're doing the best for your child by investing in everything except time together at home.

Mothers in one Bible study in an affluent area were concerned about the comments they were hearing from their kids. "You don't even have an upstairs or a basement," a mother overheard one boy tell another. A 10-year-old girl had a friend over to watch a movie; after a while her friend threw up her arms and said, "I'm going home. I can't stand to watch this. It's just not a big screen TV!" With that, she left the house.

Kids are shaped by the environment their parents establish. If yours know only privilege, they'll have little patience for "sacrificing" by watching a 27-inch television, not even thinking about how rude it is to get up and walk away.

Our actions really do speak louder than words. How you respond when your 3-year-old accidentally spills her strawberry milkshake all over the interior of your brand-new car, and when your 16-year-old has a fender bender with that same car two days later, communicates more than any talk about your values.

Kids and Jobs

Modeling a balanced, disciplined work ethic will teach your kids by example. But what about after-school jobs? Aren't they also necessary to get children ready for the "real" world?

Many parents encourage their high schoolers to work outside the home to help pay for clothes, games, trips, and college. These parents want to teach their children the value of money and the discipline of hard work. But I believe there are more important things during the school year for 16-year-olds to be focusing on: schoolwork, housework, friendships, and time with family.

The day will come soon enough for working outside the home. In the meantime, kids can learn the value of money by helping to write the checks for family bills and managing an allowance. I realize the economic realities many families face, and that many kids will work during summers to help pay for college and other expenses. But during the school year, most kids have enough going on without jumping into a year-round job.

Look at it this way: Sande and I could have allowed Hannah to flip burgers and earn $6 an hour, working five-hour shifts. Or, in lieu of that $30, we could spend an afternoon together as a family—perhaps watching a movie, going for a walk or drive, getting ice cream, even staying home and cleaning the house or cooking dinner together. At the end of that day, would I even consider trading that family time for 30 bucks?

Not a chance, pal. Not a chance.

Time Is Not Money

The saying "time is money" may be true in business, but when it comes to family life, time isn't simply as good as gold—it's better. You may bill $200 per hour at the office, but the value of that hour spent with your children is priceless.

The best thing you can give your kids is not the dirt bike, the brand-name clothes, the new car at 16. What they want and need is your *time*. Time to play together, for you to listen to their struggles and questions, to share life.

Rich or poor, we're all given the same amount of time each day. You can't buy more. You can't even really save it; you can only spend it differently.

The question is, how will you spend those 24 hours each day? How much will you give your family?

Take Advantage of Time Together

I'd just arrived home on a flight from New York to Tucson and was still feeling as if someone had run me through our dryer's permanent press cycle.

"Dad, can you drive me down to Walgreens?" Hannah asked.

"What's at Walgreens?" I responded.

"I need supplies for school."

"Sure, I'll drive you down." I was jet-lagged, but wanted to see my daughter more than I wanted to see my pillow. She'd been working at camp all summer; I'd been in New York for a few days. And how often does a father get time with his daughter?

That's a crucial question if we want homegrown children. How often *does* a parent get one-on-one time with his child? It's not as often as we might like, and for the majority the amount is downright frightening.

You don't have to look far to find mindless clutter to occupy your time: junk mail, games on your cell phone, reality television. That's why I recommend that parents take advantage of *unanticipated* opportunities with their kids. When you're in the car together, will you choose to switch on talk radio or strike up a conversation of your own? When you're sitting at the breakfast table, will you pick up the newspaper or get the latest scoop from your child? On a Sunday afternoon, will you tune in the game on the tube, or tune into your child and go outside to toss the ball around?

The question isn't so much, "How often do I get with my child?" as it is, "How often do I make the best of our moments together?"

Most of these moments are free—or at least inexpensive. Recently, while driving my 94-year-old mother back to the nursing home after a visit, I asked Lauren if she'd like to come along. She did.

"Mom," I asked, "would you like to stop and get an ice cream? Lauren, how about you?" The council convened, the vote was unanimous, and we made the detour to enjoy a little extra time together.

Most of life is composed of such mundane activities: grocery shopping, dropping off and picking up the kids from school, swinging by the bank drive-through, doing dishes after dinner. We can't let ourselves forget why we're doing those things—for our traveling companions in the minivan of life.

Those special, spontaneous moments can do far more for our children than shelling out $5,000 for a weeklong vacation at Disneyland, where you'll stand in line, pay $3.50 for a small ice cream sandwich, and come home cranky and tired. Resist the allure of brand-name clothing, the latest cars, the biggest house the bank will let you mortgage, and the hot-spot vacation destinations. All these things take a backseat to the goals of being home and being with our children.

Both the lack of money and a load of it can fight against the home-grown principle. It's a daily battle.

Every parent has to wrestle with the challenge, "Look, buddy, I said your money or your life!"

Think it over!

Let's Remember:

- Most of us in Western society are part of the upper crust of human history in terms of wealth.

- Raising a family with the home court advantage means purchasing wisely; otherwise, you'll have to leave the home to dig yourself out of debt.
- Evaluate the real cost of any purchase, which includes the intention to spend time and energy in that pursuit. The parent of the homegrown child bends his hobby around his family, rather than attempting to bend his family around his hobby.
- Families with "bucks to burn" are at a higher risk of getting pulled into the activity trap simply because they can afford it.
- Actions speak louder than words. The attitudes you hold toward possessions, money, and time strongly influence how your kids will view these.
- There are more important things during the school year for 16-year-olds to do than working outside the home: schoolwork, housework, friendships, and time with the family. Kids can learn the value of money in other ways, such as helping write checks for the family's bills and managing an allowance.
- When it comes to time, we're all given the same amount each day; the gift of your time is the greatest you can give your family.
- Take advantage of everyday opportunities—meals, chores, car rides, etc.—to build your relationship with your kids.

PART II

HOMING IN

6

It's Not What You Do, It's Who You Are

Raising Children from the Inside Out

Michael Young wasn't your ordinary homecoming king. He didn't have a throwing arm to lead the football team to a state championship; he didn't have the athletic body to make girls twitter in the hallways. While others solved physics problems, Michael took life skills classes and had a hard time adding two plus two.

An 18-year-old senior at Jefferson High School in Bloomington, Minnesota, Michael may have been developmentally delayed in math, social studies, and science. But his attitude was truly gifted.

Michael studied school yearbook photos until he knew each of the 1,700 students by name. He served as student manager of the basketball team, and rarely missed a school sporting event. Before bed each night he listened to a CD of the Jefferson band.

He's as selfless an 18-year-old as you'll find; running for homecoming king wasn't even his idea. Drew Glowa, senior class president and captain of the hockey team, talked him into it. Drew got the 75 names needed on Michael's petition and campaigned for him—even though Drew was running for homecoming king himself.

Not surprisingly—from a "home court" perspective—Michael's family has had much to do with his outlook on life. Those who know Michael's parents and older sister, Laura, say they're all "positive, so giving, so dogged in opening doors for Michael."

The thought of losing the election didn't faze Michael. In fact, he told his parents on the way to school that day that he hadn't even voted for himself. But when he found out that his fellow students had chosen him to be homecoming king, he was ecstatic. He ran around the gym, nearly dragging the homecoming queen, giving high-fives all around and wearing a grin as big as his heart.[1]

Mr. and Mrs. Young obviously did something right to raise a boy to be so positive, giving, supportive of fellow students, and enthusiastic about life. If I could define the all-American kid with a home court advantage, he would look a lot more like Michael Young than like most homecoming kings who are elected for looking good in a football jersey.

Cultivating character like Michael's takes work, but it doesn't have to be rocket science. You *can* try it at home. We did with our fourth child, Hannah, when she entered her junior year of high school. Four foreign exchange students from Germany were about to experience their first day in a U.S. classroom. Sande and I encouraged Hannah to go out of her way to make the German kids feel welcomed.

"Hannah," I said, "imagine if you were starting school today in Germany." I wanted her to empathize with those kids, in a strange place, with new families, among strangers whose language was different.

"You do what you want," I continued, "but here's what I think might be good. Go up to those kids, and not only meet and welcome them, but then go back at least a second time to each of them, reminding them what your name is, and telling them that if there's anything they don't understand or need help with, just look for Hannah."

At the end of the day, I was interested in more than how she liked her teachers and classes. I wanted to know whether she'd talked to those four kids. When it comes to her education, I care more about her servant heart than her performance in math.

For the child with a home court advantage, who you are—your character, the way you relate to people and respond to the curves life throws you—is so much more important than what you can do, what you own, or how you look.

Straight to the Heart

"Beauty is only skin deep," the saying goes. But true beauty, the kind that lasts long after the body begins to sag, goes clear to the heart. If we're not careful, we'll look at our kids and miss anything below the surface.

Just think of common chatter between an adult and a child:

"Do you have a girlfriend yet?" we ask our six-year-old nephew.

"You look so pretty!" we coo at the neighbor's 18-month-old girl.

"Oh, I'll bet you grow up to be an engineer," we say to our child as he tinkers with his tricycle.

Why does the heart so often get missed?

We're too quick to admire the throwing arm of a future NFL quarterback, the shrewdness of a someday CFO, the confident strut of tomorrow's pop singer. But without the character development of a homegrown child, that future quarterback may be settling a lawsuit over a sexual harassment charge from his college days. That CFO may be jailed because he doctored the books, losing millions of investors billions of dollars. And that pop star? She may have such a high view of marriage that she gets hitched and annulled in less than three days.

When you're counting your child's blessings, never neglect what's inside.

I don't watch a whole lot of movies; other than *The Three Amigos,* I think most of them are a waste of time. But a few carry interesting messages. One of them is *Searching for Bobby Fischer,* based on the true story of a young chess prodigy named Josh Waitzkin.

"You have a good heart," his mother tells him one night as she tucks him in, "and that's the most important thing in the world."

But later in the movie, the night before an important chess tournament, Josh's performance-obsessed father tucks his boy into bed with the words, "You won't lose, Josh."

"What if I do?" Josh speculates.

"You won't!"

"I'm afraid I might."

"Josh, they're afraid. They're terrified of you. Now you get some sleep."

"Maybe it's better not to be the best," Josh suggests. "Then you can lose and it's okay."

Which of those tuck-ins set the home court advantage? The one that acknowledged the importance of Josh's heart.

Emphasizing inner qualities isn't just a matter of future rewards, either; it has benefits now, too. Selfish but gifted children are nuisances at home. Beautiful but arrogant and lazy kids can be miserable to live with. What makes home life sweet? Good hearts, decent manners, consideration, patience, forgiveness. Those are the inner traits of a child with a home court advantage.

Ten Keys to "Home Court" Character

Is a good heart your greatest desire for your child? Or are you toeing a different line—perhaps without realizing it?

I think the latter was the case with two parents who approached me one evening. They wanted to show off their three-year-old boy's haircut—a trendy style shaved up the sides. Since a three-year-old doesn't know Vidal Sassoon from the grocery store butcher, I had to conclude that the cut wasn't for his benefit. More likely it was for the parents, who couldn't resist peer pressure to make themselves look good. Would that little boy grow up to adopt more "outside the home" values later in life?

Oh, Dr. Leman, you may say, *if our child doesn't know the difference, and we think it looks cute, what's the harm in that?*

The harm, fellow parent, won't show in your child right away. It lies in the patterns you're setting by pushing your child to be like everyone else. Rather than giving your child the home court advantage, you're having him play on everyone else's courts. Do you really want that? In case you haven't noticed, "everyone else's" child isn't doing so hot.

Cultivating homegrown character sounds good. But how can you do it in the real world? Here are 10 keys to raising your child from the inside out.

Key #1: Understand Your Child's Uniqueness

For days I observed the ducks that congregated at the edge of the lake outside our house, feeding them cracked corn when they waddled onto the grass. I was amazed to see that even with a lake full of ducklings— all of them the same to me—every mother duck seemed to somehow know her own.

I guess every duckling is different. I *know* every human is.

When your child is born, you begin unraveling the mystery of his or her uniqueness. The process might begin as you learn for sure the sex of your baby when the doctor turns that infant over and checks out the plumbing. You watch to see whether he or she is tranquil as a pond or active as a mountain waterfall. You listen and learn whether that familiar cry is from loneliness, fear, or hunger.

In time you discover whether his favorite book is *Curious George* or *The Little Engine That Could*. Later you notice whether he likes rap or jazz. You shake your head as she grows up loving astrophysics and then in college switches to creative writing, or as he transforms from being quiet as a whisper to being outspoken in politics.

The beauty of your relationship is that there's never been another quite like it. You'll always uncover new things as you spend time together. These are the "quiet discoveries" of family life, more exciting and fulfilling than anything Lewis and Clark, Christopher Columbus, or a NASA astronaut ever witnessed. You'll miss them if you're always taxiing your kids to tennis lessons or having a child care worker tuck them in for their afternoon nap.

Key #2: Give Your Kids a Piece of You

In at least one respect, dogs and kids are pretty much alike.

No matter where I am in the house, our dog Rosie insists on following me more closely than a tick. She not only sits next to me, she insists on sitting *on* me. She's a lap dog, a little cocker spaniel. She'll come bounding up with her squeaky toy dripping saliva and drop it on my clean pants.

Here's the strong similarity between Rosie and my kids: All of them want a piece of me.

Squeaky toys, doggie biscuits, even tenderloin steaks may satisfy for a while, but they'll never replace me. Yet kids and pets will take what they can get. If you allow the relationship to become about giving them car rides, buying them new video games, and just keeping them busy, they'll take that. But I believe their hearts will be wishing for you.

Parents of homegrown kids let their children have a piece of them—a good, healthy piece.

If you doubt that your child really wants to spend time with you, just ask any child whose parent took her out on "dates" if she remembers details from those one-on-one outings. You're sure to get some stories. One daughter remembers sweating through a thirteen-mile bike ride in the Florida sun with her father, but relishing it nevertheless because the two of them were alone and together. A boy remembers getting lost on a hike with his dad when he was just six years old; it was a bit scary at first, but those hours created a lifelong memory he'll cherish forever.

Key #3: Treat Each Child Differently

I once listened to four adult siblings talk among themselves after the funeral of one of their parents. Each eagerly recounted all that the deceased parent had done with him or her individually; each had secretly thought his or her relationship with that parent was the most special in the family. All were shocked to discover that their brothers and sisters had the same thought!

What a wonderful gift to each child! You can do this, too—by taking time to establish a unique relationship with each of your children.

It's easy to embrace one-size-fits-all parenting, in which certain practices are supposed to cover every personality, temperament, and disposition. As appealing as that may sound, it's simply not possible. One size may fit Al, but it doesn't fit all.

Some kids learn character best by verbal instruction; some learn by tactile involvement; others learn by seeing an example. Some are incredibly sensitive and only need a raised eyebrow in discipline; others need a firmer approach. Parents of homegrown children take time to learn the mysterious makeup of each child.

Kids thrive on the special connections that grow from this method. When Hannah and Lauren were younger, I called them by nicknames. Lauren was "my little muffin" and Hannah was "my little peanut." They ate up this "muffin" and "peanut" talk because for each of them it created a unique connection with me.

I must have been gotten my food groups mixed up one day, though. In a disastrous slip of the tongue, I called Lauren "my little peanut" and Hannah "my little muffin." Boy, did they ever make me eat *those* words! I found out just how passionately they held their special distinctions. In their minds, the mix-up was a great betrayal, like forgetting an anniversary or the details of a first date with a spouse.

To my kids, and to yours, those customized connections are markers of intimacy.

Key #4: Give Them Rituals

When our older kids were growing up, Friday mornings meant treats from the bakery. There were all sorts of goodies to choose from, which made it hard for me to decide between the turnovers, raspberry-filled doughnuts, and maple bars. But Krissy never had a problem with her order; she always asked for a little *petit four*. She requested it so regularly that it became a ritual between us.

When that tiny pastry came out of the box at home every Friday, it wasn't only the thought of how good it would taste that pleased her. It was also the fact that I'd been thinking of her when she wasn't around. We all love it when someone does something nice for us in our absence; it's a sign that we hold a cherished place in that other person's life.

When I brought that *petit four* home each week, Krissy also felt loved because she saw that I knew her and her preferences. Of course, simply knowing a list of things that your child likes isn't enough. You may know he likes baseball and pick him up a Yankees baseball cap on your way through LaGuardia during a New York business trip. But if you never throw a baseball with him nor attend his games, then that cap won't mean much because it doesn't point back to a shared life.

Kids thrive on the right kind of rituals. A review of studies (32 of them, to be exact) from the past half-century backs this homegrown approach: Family routines and rituals are "important to the health and well-being of today's busy families."[2]

Rituals often get their start without planning. Maybe you did something once that your child loved, which you've repeated until it became a routine. Your boys may have been building a fort out of sofa cushions late one afternoon when you came home from work, and you decided to wrestle them. Now they build those forts and strategize every afternoon at 4:45 P.M., waiting for your return so that they can put you in a headlock.

Keep your eyes open for your next ritual—the next thing your kids latch on to, that interaction that meets their needs and builds your homegrown bond.

Key #5: Put the Relationship First

A publisher called, wanting to reissue my book *Making Children Mind Without Losing Yours*, which first came out in 1984. Since they were repackaging the book, the publisher asked, was there anything else I might want to say in the new edition?

Funny they should ask. Over the years I've thought about adding something: Raising kids and making them mind is a lot easier than any of us make it out to be. It all comes down to one thing—the homegrown relationship you have with them.

It's as simple as that.

If your children feel they belong to your family, they have little reason from a psychological standpoint to act out. And they have good reason to listen when you try to cultivate character. So instead of trying too hard to help your children "get ahead," help them get to know you.

The authoritarian parent who says, "I'm the parent and you're going to do what I tell you to do!" isn't too interested in the relationship; he cares about getting the job done, and done well. But when you put your relationship with your child before his performance, you're preparing him from the inside out. He takes his cues from your interaction: If you're disappointed, he feels that and adjusts accordingly; if you're pleased, he knows he's on the right track and thrives.

That leads to character development. Encourage this process by building a solid relationship in which your kids know you know them and love them—and even *like* them.

Key #6: Get Real

One day our daughter Lauren and I were in the pool, floating on our blow-up plastic pool toy. Lauren is very modest in her dress, and at 11 is conscious that her body is starting to change. Wanting her to know that she wasn't the only one who'd faced embarrassment, I brought up my own pubescent experience in swimming class—which I would have done *anything* to get out of.

"When Daddy was in seventh and eighth grade," I said, "we had to swim in the nude during swimming class."

"What?" Lauren asked, shocked.

"We didn't have swimming suits," I replied.

"You mean you went in . . . *bare*?" she asked.

"Yeah."

"What was that like?"

"It was terrible," I replied. "I had to sit on the edge of the pool with all the other boys in my gym class—probably 30 or so—while they took attendance. Then we were in the pool for a 50-minute period, and they were sticklers about making you do it."

Sometimes parenting involves sharing some pretty painful memories. When those times come, get real: Share the uncertainty, the regret, and even your own mistakes.

Cultivating character doesn't mean faking it. Your children will discover you're not perfect if they haven't already, so don't maintain that façade. Standing in for God might be a much more enjoyable role to play, especially if you're ashamed of the times you were mischievous or dishonest. But hiding those incidents won't help your children deal with their own imperfections.

Talk about your downs as well as your ups. I don't mean sharing sordid details. But as you communicate that you, too, have experienced problems in life, that will help them know they're not alone.

Maintaining a godlike persona will only distance your child as he realizes he's made of more mortal stuff. The essence of developing intimacy with your kids is telling them who you really are, and giving them the opportunity to tell you who they really are.

I'm not talking about trying to be your child's best buddy. He or she needs your parental experience and wisdom. But talking with your kids about uncomfortable subjects as naturally as you can will help them find comfort in discussing subjects *they* feel uncomfortable about.

Key #7: Nurture Their Trust

If your child opens her heart and tells you something confidential, don't run over it or make fun of it. If she tells you that she doesn't feel she fits in at school, don't dismiss it by saying, "Honey, you shouldn't worry about that!" If he asks, "Dad, what's a condom?" don't strike down the question by saying, "We don't talk about things like that!" Take these in stride; hear them out; take your child's heart seriously.

Your child's vulnerability is a sign of intimacy. That's what you work toward as a parent; don't brush it aside or, worse, belittle it. Take the vulnerable moments as a gift, the gift of a growing relationship which is a prerequisite for building character.

Many say close relationships with sons and daughters can't be had, or make frustrated jokes about the gap between generations. Don't despair. You may not wear the latest fashions, but if you guard your child's trust, close family relationships never have to go out of style!

Key #8: Model Values Worth Catching

I was in line to grab a burger at the local Wendy's. The son of the man in front of me walked over from the table where the rest of the family sat. I couldn't hear the little boy's question, but I had no problem hearing the father's response.

"Well, you tell your mother that if she wants something she can just come over and get it!" he snapped.

I wondered, *What kind of husband is that little boy going to be someday? How will he treat women? When his wife asks him if he'll bring napkins from the kitchen, will he follow what his daddy taught him?*

I ordered my meal, glad that my daughters weren't there to hear the man's outburst. Had they been, I would have said to them, "There are people in life who talk like that, people who disrespect their kids by screaming at them. Your job is to find someone who is not like that."

Values really are caught, not taught. Your kids are watching your every move, taking mental notes. The beliefs and behavior you model are the foundation on which your children's character is built; the way you see your children is the way they'll see themselves.

Respect your kids and they'll see themselves as respectable. Be gracious with them and they'll learn grace themselves. Listen to them and they'll grow up listening to others and believing they have a voice worth hearing.

Key #9: Use Chores to Teach

My wife, Sande, once threw a banana peel on the kitchen floor and left it there to see what the rest of us would do. Our kids walked by and looked at it. *Oh,* you can imagine them thinking, *someone's getting in trouble.*

Later that day Sande asked, "Did anyone notice the banana peel on the kitchen floor? I know you all walked by it."

You tell them, Sande, I thought. *What were you thinking, kids? I thought we taught you better than that.*

"But *you,*" she said, turning to me, "*you* looked at it, kicked it aside with your foot, and kept right on going."

Oh.

I got in *big* trouble that time, the psychologist failing the psychology experiment. Apparently, through my own example, I *hadn't* taught them better than that.

Most of us, parent and child alike, have thought at one time or another, *That's not my job.* Sometimes it's not. But I'm always pleased to see customers in the grocery store picking up cereal boxes that have tipped off the shelves or apples that have rolled to the produce section floor. When I see an accident like that, I stop to help. If the kids are with me, they learn more about chipping in than they would from any lecture.

It sounds old-fashioned, but chores can teach character. Keep a few cautions in mind, though:

• Make jobs age-appropriate. Don't ask kids to hand wash your crystal at age four—and then scream when they drop an expensive piece.

- Have kids work in different areas of the house—avoiding conflict between Bobby cleaning the toilet and Susie cleaning the bathroom sink, for example.
- Change kids' jobs occasionally; there's nothing worse than being the garbage person for life.
- If you want a job done right, do it yourself—but I'm talking about parenting, not sweeping the floor. If you want to teach your two-year-old daughter to pitch in, give her a broom and dustpan and a lot of slack. Don't stand over her like a field marshal and criticize her work. For kids ages two to four it's much more important that they learn enthusiasm for helping than that they make the kitchen floor sparkle.

Key #10: Look Out for Others

"Why do you stop at stop signs?" I often ask people.

Most will answer, "So I don't get in an accident." Others may say, "It's the law." Those are pretty good reasons. But I hope that we also stop at stop signs so that we don't hurt other people.

It's easy to start with Number One and move outward from there. But what a wonderful gift when you can instill in your child a heart that looks out for others first. That's the way to nurture that home court advantage.

To cultivate selflessness, enlist the family's participation. If a storm lashes the neighborhood and scatters debris over the yard, cleaning the mess isn't Mother Nature's job—and Father Time isn't going to be much help in the near future.

I wouldn't ask the kids, "Would you like to help Mommy?" Given the choice of picking up the yard or playing with a friend, you're not going to hear, "Oh, really, can we, Mom?" Most kids aren't waiting eagerly for a cue to help; they need gentle direction until they learn over time that pitching in is expected.

I would instead say, "Come on, everybody to the backyard. We all need to pick this up now."

That positive expectation communicates a message: We work together as a family and look out for the needs around us.

An Inside Job

Parents of kids with a home court advantage focus on the inside of the child, not the outside. They know that what's inside—character—makes the most difference in the long run.

Does your child understand that? Now's the time to make it clear, through your relationship and the time you take to know him, focus on his unique qualities, and nurture him from the inside out.

Let's Remember:

- It's not what you do, it's who you are that matters.
- When you draw your esteem from what your children do outside the home, you'll be lured into emphasizing things the world most covets: ability, good looks, and charisma.
- Do you want your child to be like everyone else? Then be prepared for a rocky life! Every child is unique, and your job as a parent is to discover and nurture individual traits.
- Spend focused, individual time with your children so that each one feels he or she is the most important child in the family.
- Kids thrive on special connections and rituals. Because rituals

often grow naturally out of interaction, keep your eyes open for interaction that especially meets your kids' needs.

- When you find opportunities to tell your kids about your life in ways that help them with theirs, get real: Share the uncertainty, the pain, and even your own mistakes.
- Nurture your child's trust. If your child opens her heart and tells you something confidential, don't run over it or make fun of it.
- Values are caught, not taught. Your kids are watching your every move. What you model serves as the foundation on which your children's character is built.
- More important than managing family chores and maintaining a spotless house is nurturing your child's willingness to pitch in. Model a healthy response to the needs around you at home and in public, and draw your children into shared family responsibility.

What Mayberry's Sheriff Andy Taylor Taught Me

. . . About the Home Court Advantage

I love *The Andy Griffith Show.* The TV series combined lovable characters and entertaining story lines with positive life lessons, and it's still rerun today. The lessons that Sheriff Andy Taylor teaches his son, Opie, still serve parents well.

One of my favorite episodes[1] focuses on nurturing and believing in your child, come what may, which is essential if you want that home court advantage.

As the story begins, Opie is the proud owner of a new slingshot and is anxious to get outside to try it. Andy cautions his son to be careful with it, and Opie promises to shoot only at tin cans and such things.

He heads down the sidewalk, taking shots at bushes and tree trunks. Suddenly he spots movement in a tree and sends a stone flying, hitting a bird and knocking it to the ground.

Slowly, Opie approaches in stunned disbelief. As the bird lies motionless, the boy puts the slingshot in his back pocket, kneels down, and scoops the creature into his hands.

"Fly away," Opie cries. "*Please* fly away!" Gently he tosses the bird into the air to help it take off, but it falls lifeless to the grass.

Crying, Opie turns and runs inside.

Later that afternoon, Andy returns home. When he picks up the newspaper from the sidewalk, he sees the dead bird and hears baby birds in the nearby tree. He peers up at the nest with a knowing look.

At supper that evening, as Opie picks at his food, Andy remarks to Aunt Bee that their neighbor ought to keep her cat inside because it had killed one of their songbirds.

That wasn't possible, Aunt Bee replies. Mrs. Snyder was gone for over a week and had taken her cat with her.

Opie leaves the table and rushes upstairs.

Is he sick? Aunt Bee wonders out loud. Andy, however, knows better and follows Opie upstairs to the boy's room.

"You killed that bird, didn't you?" Andy asks.

Opie is at first silent, then nods.

Andy sternly reminds his son about his warning earlier in the day to be careful with the slingshot, and Opie says he is sorry.

"That won't bring that bird back to life," Andy points out. "Being sorry is not the magic word that makes everything right again."

Opie asks if he's going to get a "whippin'," but Andy shakes his head.

Instead, Andy makes a wise move. He simply walks across the room and opens the window. Outside on a nearby branch sits the nest with the motherless baby birds, whose hungry peeps fill the room.

"You hear that?" Andy says. "That's those young birds chirping for their momma that's never coming back. Now you just listen to that for a while."

What Andy has used with Opie is what I call "reality discipline." That's the principle of letting the natural consequences of your child's actions discipline him or her—in this case, considering how shooting the mother bird has affected those baby birds. It allows for the reality of the situation to be the best teacher to the child.

Every decision we make has consequences. If you let those natural results teach your child rather than using arbitrary reward and punishment, you'll be preparing your child to live responsibly—which is one mark of a kid with a home court advantage.

External Control vs. Internal Guidance

Reality discipline helps kids develop internal guidance systems rather than just controlling their actions. As a parent, my job is not to control my child. Not even God controls us. He doesn't reach down, push us against a wall, and say, "You *will* acknowledge Me."

Not that some parents don't try. Sande and I knew a guy whose kids sat on our couch like birds on a fence—legs crossed and hands folded as they waited for their father to give them permission to move! Those aren't homegrown children; they're puppets yanked around by rules.

Kids who are easily controlled are pushovers for their peer group. I want my child to learn to say *no* when told to "drink this, shoot this, snort this." That kind of training is done primarily from the inside out.

Discipline may be something I do "to" my daughter, but it's also something I nurture in her so that she learns to make wise decisions herself. Inner discipline is infinitely more important than outer conformity, especially when your child turns 18 and leaves home. When you're no longer around to set the rules, what kind of character and self-discipline will he or she exercise?

That's why it wouldn't be a good idea to tell Opie, "Here's your new slingshot. Now, if you shoot the birds or the neighbors' windows, I'm going to take it away and ground you for a week!" Sure, you need to assess the boy's maturity to handle the slingshot and remind him to be careful. But if you threaten him with punishment before he's even pulled back the sling, you've said to him, *This slingshot is probably more than you can handle, so when [not if] you mess up, here's what you'll have coming to you.*

That isn't reality discipline. It's the kind of traditional discipline that hasn't worked for years. It uses fear of punishment to get the child to conform on the outside; reality discipline works through natural consequences, mutual respect, and a belief in the best that is in your child. Emphasizing the latter helps your child develop those character traits on the home court.

The Truth about Consequences

By letting Opie experience the consequences of his actions, Andy has helped the boy understand the relationship between his decisions and their effects on him and those around him. If Andy had given him "a whippin'," Opie may have gotten the message that he should listen to his dad more carefully next time. But as a child grows, punishment loses its sting; the day comes when Dad and Mom aren't there to administer the consequences. What then?

The nice thing about childhood is that consequences are rather tame compared to those later in life. Cheating on the seventh grade math test has fewer consequences than cheating on income taxes. By allowing Opie to suffer consequences when the stakes are lower, Andy is nurturing in Opie an inner responsibility that will help prevent more painful consequences down the road.

So when should you use consequences as part of raising kids?

Believe it or not, the teachable moment doesn't have to happen right after your child doesn't do what he's supposed to, or tells the lie, or comes home late.

Let's say your daughter smart-mouths you. Two hours later she wants to be driven to the mall to meet her friends. You might reply, "I don't feel like driving you to the mall today."

"*Mom*," your child might say, "I just want to go to the mall!"

"Honey," you could reply, "you're not hearing what I'm saying. I don't feel like doing it today."

That kid will not give up, and pretty soon you'll have an opportunity to tell her straight out what is on your mind.

"Well, to be specific, I'm still not happy about the way you talked to me around 9:30 this morning when I asked you to take the garbage out and check on your baby brother. I didn't like your attitude, I didn't like the look on your face, and I certainly didn't appreciate the words you uttered under your breath—that I did hear, by the way."

For the two of you to reconcile, that daughter has to acknowledge her wrongdoing. Otherwise, the natural consequence is a rift in your relationship.

After the Consequences

Let's return to Opie's story for a look at what should happen *after* using consequences.

Once Andy has let Opie sit with the results of his actions, he doesn't prolong the lesson the following day out of anger. He allows a new day to bring a new start marked by grace. Rather than laying into the boy all over again for his mistake, Andy warmly wishes him, "Mornin', son."

Opie is sitting on the porch steps with a box cradled in his lap. Curious, Andy asks what the boy is doing. Opie replies that he's fixing breakfast for the baby birds that he has adopted and named Winkin', Blinkin', and Nod. When Aunt Bee comes out onto the porch a few minutes later, Andy tells her that Opie is owning up to the consequences of his actions by mothering the baby birds.

You see, not only does Andy follow his reality discipline with a fresh start for Opie, he also affirms the change in his son in the responsibility the boy shows by taking care of the hatchlings.

If you care for those baby birds well, Andy tells Opie after he has fed them for a few days, you'll be proud of them when they're grown. It's a message that echoes what we're talking about regarding the home court advantage for your children. When you focus on raising your kids as well as you can—nurturing them by giving them responsibility, holding them accountable for their actions, and showing them grace when they fail—then in all probability they'll grow to be mature and responsible, the kind of kids you hope they might be.

Most parents tend to direct praise at their children's behavior: "My, you're a good boy because you played so nicely with your friends this afternoon." The child assumes she's held in high esteem because she did well. But it's much more important to acknowledge kids for who they are than for what they've done. The parent of a homegrown child cares less about performance and more about the attitude he or she has when trying.

An encouraging statement might be, "Now you're getting it!" or "It looks like that extra practice is really paying off!"

When I'm asked to describe my kids, you'll hear me say things such as, "They sincerely care about other people." I'm so proud of who my daughter *is*: her giving nature, the way she relates to people. I try to notice those traits and encourage them as best I can, to let her know Dad is watching.

As Opie releases Winkin', Blinkin', and Nod at the end of the episode, he breathes a sigh of relief that the birds all flew off okay. Andy affirms the efforts of his son, who then looks back down with a touch of loss.

The cage looks so empty, Opie says.

Andy agrees, but then wisely adds a final note of encouragement: "But don't the trees seem nice and full?" he says as birdsong fills the yard.

The home court is a place of grace, of second chances. It's also a place where the right attitudes are encouraged through the right kind of praise.

Believe in Your Child

Will you indulge me by letting me use another episode of *The Andy Griffith Show*? I honestly think this series should be part of every child's elementary education—and probably part of every parent's education in raising children.

In another favorite episode of mine,[2] Opie tells Andy and Deputy Barney Fife that he met a man named Mr. McBeevee who "walks around up in the treetops." He wears a "great, big, shiny silver hat," says Opie, and "he sort of jingles" when he walks, "just like he had rings on his fingers and bells on his toes." That comes "from all the things hanging on his belt" and his "twelve extra hands." To top it off, Opie tells his dad and Barney that Mr. McBeevee can "make smoke come out of his ears."

He even gave me a quarter, Opie adds, pulling the coin from his shirt pocket.

Andy, who has been listening to his son with amusement, asks if what he just heard was correct: that Mr. McBeevee, the fellow Opie had just described in the most outlandish terms, gave him the quarter.

Sure, Opie tells his father, as naturally as if men in trees handed out quarters every day. Mr. McBeevee said he'd earned it.

Andy, who is now bewildered, asks where Opie *really* got the quarter.

Opie stands by his answer: Mr. McBeevee. If his dad would like to hear it from Mr. McBeevee himself they should go to the woods together and ask *him* to tell his father the story.

Andy, who is now uncomfortable with Opie's tall tale and wants to get to the bottom of it, takes him up on the idea and the two of them set off.

Once they reach the woods, Opie calls up into the trees for Mr. McBeevee, begging him to come down and tell his father about the quarter.

As you might expect, there is no reply.

The two wander through the forest as Opie calls again and again up into the trees for Mr. McBeevee. But still there is no response.

Finally, Andy tells Opie it's time to head home.

Back in Opie's bedroom, Andy confronts his son regarding the difference between make-believe stories and the truth. He reminds Opie of the fun the two of them were having that morning talking about Opie's make-believe horse, "Blackie," and points out that Blackie was simply made up from the boy's imagination.

Perhaps the same was true for Mr. McBeevee, Andy suggests. Perhaps Mr. McBeevee was also made up for fun. Andy is quick to note that there's nothing wrong with that, as long as what we imagine doesn't get in the way of our responsibilities and cause us to avoid what really happened. He then tells Opie that at times the responsible thing to do is to own up to reality rather than hiding behind what we imagine to be true.

All Opie has to do, says Andy, is admit that Mr. McBeevee is make-believe and the whole incident will be forgotten. But if he doesn't, Andy adds, he thinks Opie knows what is coming.

Opie begins to deny Mr. McBeevee, but then stops.

"I can't, Pa. Mr. McBeevee isn't make-believe. He's real."

"*Opie . . .*" begins Andy.

"Don't you believe me, Pa?" Opie pleads. "Don't you, Pa?"

Andy considers his son for a moment, then sighs.

He nods his head. "I believe you," he says. He pats Opie on the leg, leaves his room, and walks downstairs to where Barney Fife and Aunt Bee are waiting.

Barney is at first relieved that Opie didn't receive a spanking, but when he hears that Andy told Opie that he believed him, the deputy is beside himself. What Opie is saying is *impossible*, Barney declares.

Andy points out that many times he tells Opie to believe things that must seem impossible to his son. He certainly has a point; it must be difficult for a young child to accept that strangers offering candy are up to no good, and that discipline is for his or her best.

But, Barney protests, what about all that talk about Mr. McBeevee's silver hat and how he jingles when he walks?

Andy isn't sure what to make of it all, but he says that at times you have to decide whether or not to take a step of faith to believe in someone.

"But you do believe in Mr. McBeevee?" asks Barney.

"No, no," Andy says thoughtfully. "I do believe in Opie."

Though Opie's story seems completely fantastical, Sheriff Taylor takes an admirable step. He believes in his son in spite of all the evidence to the contrary.

I can't underscore enough the importance of believing in your child, come flunking grades or being on a first-name basis in the principal's office. Believing in your child is one of the best investments you can make; your confidence inspires him to move toward your vision of what he can be. When you communicate by your words and actions, "I believe in you and expect the best of you," kids strive to honor that.

When Opie Lets You Down

At the end of that episode, Andy heads back into the woods to mull over Opie's insistence that Mr. McBeevee is real. Shaking his head, he says Mr. McBeevee's name out loud in disbelief—and is astonished to hear someone answer from above! Seconds later, a man climbs down one of the trees using spiked boots. He's a telephone lineman, and when he reaches the ground he introduces himself as Mr. McBeevee.

Andy stands there in wonder. "You walk around in the trees. Silver hat. You jingle," he says, looking at his tool belt. "You can make smoke come out of your ears, can't you? Mr. McBeevee, I can't tell you how glad I am to meet you!" Andy shakes the man's hand vigorously. "I'm Andy Taylor, Opie's dad!"

Well, you may think, *Andy's belief in his child paid off* that *time.*

But even if Opie *had* been lying, that belief would have paid off. It would have touched the boy's desire to live up to his father's expectations—and triggered disappointment in letting his dad down.

Let's assume for a moment that you take Sheriff Taylor's approach—and it turns out that your child is making the whole thing up. Mr. McBeevee is a complete fabrication, and your little rascal knows it. What should you do?

When your kid tells you what you know for a fact is a whopper, you might say, "So, your friend Steven saw Mr. McBeevee, too? I think I'll call Steven's mother right now and ask her about that." Get down to where the rubber meets the road. There's a consequence for his lying:

your broken trust and the guilt he feels for having disappointed you—as well as his embarrassment at having his lie exposed.

Here's something else you might do. Next time he asks to go someplace he goes every day after school, tell him *no*.

"No?" he'll ask, surprised. "Why no? You always let me go there."

"There's no reason for me to believe you'll *be* there," you could reply.

"What do you mean? I *always* go there."

"Well, do you remember what you said about Mr. McBeevee? If I couldn't trust you then, why should I trust you now? You're going to have to build up your credibility again. So the answer today is *no*."

That's how I'd handle it so that he sees there's a consequence for lying. But once your child's failure is in the open, don't carry on. Remember the need for grace and encouragement.

Many people won't believe in your child. If there's one person left standing in the world who does, that person should be you.

And that, among other things, is what I learned in Mayberry.

Let's Remember:

- Reality discipline—the act of letting natural consequences teach your child—helps prepare her to live responsibly.
- Let the reality of the situation become a teachable moment for your child.
- Discipline is more than something you *do* to your children; more importantly, it's something you nurture inside them so that they learn to make wise decisions.
- Believe in your child. It's one of the best investments you can make as a parent, because your confidence inspires him to move toward your vision of what he can be.

- Once your child's failure is in the open, don't carry on. Don't shame him into a corner; calmly but firmly express your disappointment. Your composure and the underlying belief that his failure does not define him will speak volumes.

The Power of Positive Expectations

Agustin began parenting his newborn son, fresh from the hospital, as if the boy were cramming for a final. The schedule included incessant reading, music by Mozart and Beethoven, and hours together watching educational TV programs. The man had great hopes for his son.

Agustin had written a short story about a gifted child who grew up to become a scientist and world leader in an intergalactic movement to help humankind. He'd also developed a "Magic Formula," a "secret technique designed to accelerate the energy in fertile women so as to produce gifted children," and gave this formula to his live-in partner, Cathy.

At just six and a half weeks of age, Adragon (named in honor of the Chinese Year of the Dragon) allegedly spoke his first word: *hello*. At age three the boy was studying math problems. At age five, his IQ was 400—at least according to Agustin's testing—which would have made him perhaps the greatest intellect in history.

Adragon was only eight when he entered Cabrillo College, where he reportedly learned calculus by age nine—three years ahead of Einstein. At age 10 he transferred to UC Santa Cruz to pursue computational mathematics, enrolling for double the normal student load. He graduated a year later, the youngest college graduate ever according to the *Guinness Book of World Records*.

In interviews, Agustin called Adragon "his 'greatest creation' and 'probably the most unique child that any generation has seen since the time of Da Vinci.'"

Agustin saw Adragon's time with friends, however, as wasted—a point on which he and Cathy disagreed. After school he would "whisk the poor kid away and rush him home to cram more facts in his head," said Lewis Keizer, director of the Popper-Keizer School for gifted children, where Adragon was enrolled for a short time.

On September 19, 1988, law enforcement officers stormed Agustin's house with a warrant "based on an affidavit signed by AD's mother: Agustin's 'Grand Plan' for AD amounted to child abuse; AD was in danger; Agustin possessed a cache of weapons; AD would be better served living with her." Officers snatched Adragon from the house, away from Agustin and his "Grand Plan."

Today achievement is no longer the most important thing in Adragon's life. Friends are, he says. Known by those friends simply as "James," the former prodigy still loves his father deeply.

Learning how to be a kid, though, has been a major adjustment. That, admits James, "might be harder than calculus."[1]

Was Agustin wrong to have dreams for his child? Doesn't everyone, child and adult, dream of something?

I still remember as a Little Leaguer walking up to home plate, hoping to plaster the ball out of the park, and hearing my father yell his dream from the stands: "Hit a home run!"

Those words echoing in my mind made me much more desperate to connect with the ball.

Which brings me to the clash of two very common dreams—a child's dream of pleasing his parents, and a parent's dream that her kids will experience the life she wants them to. It's a conflict we need to address if we want our kids to benefit from the home court advantage.

Sweet Dreams?

Our childhood experiences and adult hopes tend to color how we encourage—or discourage—our kids as they grow. If athletics was your ticket to popularity in school, you may find yourself pushing your child into sports when he or she is content with chess club. You may remember the sting of failing to make it into law school, so you drive your child to make it through that door.

Many of our dreams are healthy; we want our children to receive a good education, to grow in love, and to be accepted by others. But when our dreams clash with their personalities, or hone their abilities to the neglect of their healthy development in other areas, we're stepping out of line. Kids want parents' affirmation; unfortunately, if you have your own "Grand Plan" in motion, they're likely to go along with it.

In contrast is one mother I talked to who has a delightful "home-grown" perspective. Her nine-year-old daughter had a singing role in a Christmas play. The girl practiced and practiced—but when she got up to perform, she bungled the words badly. Though she carried on courageously, she began crying as soon as she was offstage.

The mother encouraged her daughter but told me in private, "I was so pleased to see this happen. I had been praying for something like this. Because of her personality, she needs to learn how to deal with failure a little bit better. I was just thankful that I could be there so we could talk about it."

This mom has her priorities straight. She values building character over a performance no one will remember three weeks from now. She also made sure she was there to witness it, which gave her the chance to offer immediate, helpful input.

What's Your Dream?

Where do you want your child to be at age 18? More to the point, *who* do you want your child to be? Do you envision a charismatic 4.0 scholar with Ivy League schools clamoring for his admission? How about at age 22? A professional athlete? A highly paid attorney straight out of law school?

Many parents won't admit such things, but their actions make it obvious what they're aiming for. To reach these destinations, some parents will do anything—including their kids' homework. Roughly one-fourth of parents admit to occasionally doing their child's homework when their child is too tired or the work is too hard.[2]

As a counselor, I find that many parental expectations are born of good intentions. One man might buck his family history, working his way through high school and college to become a successful business-man. Not wanting his children to fall back into the life he escaped, he pushes them to achieve—until he pushes them right out of his life.

Or a mother, feeling she married "beneath" herself, wants to spare her daughter that fate. The woman harps on the girl's posture, dress, exercise, and general hygiene—missing the point that a good marriage depends almost entirely on character and has almost nothing to do with appearance.

Parents of homegrown children take stock of their own experiences in order to avoid repeating hurtful patterns with their children. Take a moment to reflect on your own childhood and the corresponding expectations you have for your kids.

Most of us run from these hurts: *That was so long ago, Dr. Leman. Why should I revisit painful memories?* So that you don't saddle your children with those same memories!

Honestly ask yourself: How have my childhood disappointments and losses influenced the expectations I have for my children today? How does my desire to look like a good and competent parent put even more pressure on my kids? Know yourself, because that self-awareness can temper your tendency to push your children in ways that might not even seem like pushing to you.

Here's an example. One of the most common irritations kids express to me in the counseling room is that they're forever being compared to siblings and friends. Practically all parents are guilty of this from time to time; it can be so subtle:

"Remember when Johnny first did that?" you might ask your spouse when your little daughter shows you her somersault.

Without meaning to, you've just told your child, "Your older brother did that three years earlier than you did. What's the big deal?"

Comparisons are always misleading because no two kids will ever be exactly alike. This is a big world; we need analytical people, funny people, managers, athletes, followers, leaders, you name it. What does it matter if second-born Samuel isn't as quick with numbers as first-born Alan? If Sammy becomes a talk-show host, he can *hire* people like Alan to keep his books. Parents of homegrown children realize that it takes all kinds, so they accept and nurture their children's gifts as they come.

Your dreams should be in line with God's design and gifting for your girl or boy. Chuck Swindoll told me that you could translate Proverbs 22:6, "Train a child in the way he should go," as "train a child *according to his bent.*"

Your life is your life; your past is your past. Don't ask your child to carry it. Set your kids free to become the people God made them to be.

Blowouts and Slow Leaks

Most kids aren't all that adept at articulating their emotions. They won't come up to you and say, "Can we talk? I'm just feeling that I can never measure up to what you want me to be. So I'm considering getting argumentative over petty things, disrupting family activities, and picking on my little sister because you're expecting the world of me."

A kid's not going to say that—but if that's how he feels, you'll probably see it in his behavior. He may start getting mouthy with one or both parents; if an outsider were to watch him for a few days, he might say, "You have an angry kid."

My advice: Don't ignore the emotional duress. Dr. James Dobson calls this the "Blowout vs. the Slow Leak Syndrome." If you've built up tension over the years between you and your child due to your expectations, don't let it leak into his adult years. Having a homegrown child means addressing the tension now—and doing so sensitively, making changes and discussing them as needed over the coming months. There's no harm in moving carefully; by "blowout" I don't mean "blow up"!

You don't have to make radical changes overnight. Perhaps start with an apology; doing so will probably help avoid bloodshed! "Honey, I'm sorry," you might tell your daughter. "Moms and dads make mistakes, too. I think I've been too hard on you and I'm sorry. I want you to know how proud I am of you."

Thank Goodness They're Normal!

A well-known Bible teacher once pointed out that when a child is in the womb we pray for nine months that he'll emerge looking normal. Then, even if he does, we never accept normal again! We want him to forever rise above the average.

For every "success" story—say, an inner-city boy who made it out of the ghetto and bought a new home for his mom—I could tell you a dozen about a suburbanite who bent her entire family around a daughter's potential gymnastics career, only to discover her little girl didn't have what it took to compete on a national level. Or a mom who woke all her kids up early Saturday mornings to take the oldest boy to his swim meets in another town—and then became bitter when junior decided he wanted to race motorcycles instead.

There's something wonderful about having a normal, average kid who doesn't feel pressured to be the top student in class or a starting quarterback. In my high school class there were some we all thought would make it big in the "real world," but they didn't go much further than the school parking lot. If your child is average, celebrate. I'm so glad I have normal kids, kids who enjoy life, feel good about themselves, and give generously to other people.

Those inner qualities of kids with a home court advantage are worth much more to me than any string of A's or seeing my child's face flash across ESPN.

Seven Ways to Use Positive Expectations

So much about setting the bar too high. How do you hit the mark when it comes to expectations?

Let's talk about the power of positive expectations in the process of raising kids on the home court.

Way #1: Give Them Amazing Grace

Occasionally when I'm asked to speak at a church, I'll do a little role-playing. I'm a shepherd and the congregation is my flock.

"All right, sheep," I'll say. "I was just listening to KIRO radio and the weather's changing, so it's time to hightail it to better pasture. Let's move out!"

There are always a few who don't want to play along. People at church don't expect to move much when the guy up front is talking.

What would a good shepherd do in a case like this? He'd give the sheep a little tap on the side and they'd fall back into line. He wouldn't beat them into submission; a little tap would do.

That's the way it is with kids with a home court advantage. You're the shepherd and your children are your sheep. Many view a shepherd's rod and staff as instruments of punishment and pain, but the Bible says the rod and staff *comfort*.[3] The rod, in fact, was used for rescuing and protecting, not to wallop the animals black and blue.

Positive expectation is full of grace: it allows for failure. When Junior whines for a candy bar in the grocery store, expecting the best allows you not to panic. You say, "Silly you! Don't you remember we just discussed that?" and move on. Don't make it a bigger deal than it is. Maybe he really did forget your chat outside the supermarket. Your challenge is to assume the best and act on that.

"Nice try," the gracious parent might say when a child misses the mark. "There's always next time." Your child will get off center occasionally; when needed, you can tap him back on track. The important thing isn't that he's walking exactly in the center of the path, but that he's going in the right direction—developing the inner responsibility of a child.

Do *you* always make the right choice, respond to others in the right tone of voice, or behave your best? None of us does. Positive expectations give Junior a little space to be human.

Way #2: Build Boundaries

Positive expectations serve as guardrails on that wide path your child must travel. Let's go back to the grocery store example. Using positive expectations, you've made it clear when your kids can and can't have candy. It's normal—not rebellion—when they test you on this, asking to buy a Super Sugar Sucker to eat on your way home to cook dinner. Just smile and say, "Nice try, honey. You *know* I'm not going to let you have that, don't you?"

Little Missy smiles, maybe laughs, and puts the sucker down. Yes, she does know the boundaries. There are times she can have candy, and times she can't. She understands the boundaries, and she appreciates the fact that you talk to her as if she does: "You *know* I'm not going to let you have that, don't you?"

You can even laugh with her: "Are you being silly? Maybe we should buy lots of potato chips, too, and chocolate milk, and ice cream, and eat them in the car; then we'll be *really* hungry for dinner, won't we?"

A mom with negative expectations might meet the request for that Super Sugar Sucker, fearing she's about to face another public scene. Or she might refuse, everything about her demeanor screaming panic: "Put that down! Don't ask me again! What were you thinking? What's the matter with you? Didn't I already tell you 'no' in the car? Have you lost your hearing?"

The child recognizes that Mom is getting pretty uptight about a simple request, and all of a sudden it dawns on her: "Hey, if I'm not mistaken, I've found a chink in her armor. Let's see how far we can take this thing."

Do positive expectations help build boundaries with teenagers, too? I'm glad you asked.

"Dad," my son, Kevin II, said as he headed out one evening, "I'll be down at Peter Piper Pizza with some friends."

"Sure," I said, "have fun. Just get back at a reasonable hour."

"A reasonable hour?" he asked. "When's a reasonable hour?"

That's a question I've never answered straight out. "Oh, you know," I might reply, "a reasonable hour."

Dr. Leman, you might think, *are you nuts? You don't get much more of an open door than that!* It's true that many parents would be thrilled if their kids asked what time they needed to return at night—and you can bet they'd tell them! But the parent of a homegrown child is after more than maintaining an orderly household; he's after long-term training in character.

When is a reasonable hour? Obviously it isn't 4:00 A.M. Here in Tucson, we have public curfews; if Kevin II returned then, privileges with the car would end quickly. I wanted him to decide when a realistic hour was.

If I were to tell my son that he needed to be home at 11:00 P.M., the final line would be drawn. He might *want* to stay out later, but what would keep him from doing so? The line *I* drew. I want to train my kids from the inside out, so that the lines *they* draw help them embrace what's good and loving—and keep them from doing what hurts them and others.

The goal is to let kids learn inner responsibility at home. The trick is giving them enough freedom to decide for themselves. It's important to keep the proverbial tennis ball of life in their court. Expecting the best helps you do that.

Way #3: Play on Your Child's Team

One of our 11-year-old daughter Lauren's biggest treats is having friends over. I try to be mindful of that question forever dancing in her brain: "Can I have someone over?" I do as much as I can to give her what she honestly needs; in other words, I play on her team.

Families with negative expectations become hostile rivals, each side warily circling the other, looking for a weakness to exploit. It's much healthier to be on each other's team.

Would you say you're on your child's team? Would your child?

Being on your children's team doesn't mean dropping everything for them; you simply try to help meet their real, honest-to-goodness needs whenever you can. That's important if your children are going to have the home court advantage; remember, it all comes back to the relationship. You can't have an intimate relationship if you're constantly circling each other in the family ring, looking for a take-down hold.

If your kids see you going out of your way to meet legitimate needs, they won't be so quick to throw tantrums when you occasionally must say "no." But when you find yourself saying "no" to almost everything they ask, you don't have a home with healthy boundaries; you have a war zone with occasional cease-fires.

Way #4: Learn from Failure

I recently received a letter from my high school stating that I'd been elected to its "Wall of Fame." That was one of the funniest things I'd ever heard, because my only claim to fame in high school was my unbroken record of poor grades.

I graduated fourth from the bottom of my class. My high school counselor told me he couldn't get me in reform school. I applied to 160 colleges and universities and none of them wanted me. Not only was I a terrible student, I was a discipline problem.

But I couldn't wait to tell my mother about this post-graduation honor. After all, she was the one who went to school and talked to the teachers when I repeatedly skipped classes.

"Ma," I said, after I had read her the letter, "I guess we came out on top of that one, didn't we? We sure got the last laugh." And we did. My 92-year-old mother nearly laughed her dentures out as we talked about me going back to accept my award.

Parents who establish a home court advantage know that failure is simply an indicator that a child needs more time to develop. If your child is going to fail—and roughly 100 percent do—you want him or her to learn to fail gracefully in the safety of your home. Kids need that place to mispronounce words, say ridiculously stupid things (one girl I know wondered how they made ice cubes in Australia, since it was so hot), or try a clothes combination that only a clown would love. The "home court" family expects failure as well as success; it treats failure as a stepping-stone instead of a shameful roadblock.

Kids often say, "I can't do that. It's too hard." Many are simply more afraid of the stigma of failure than they are of testing their abilities. When your kids say things like that, gently pull them aside and say, "Hey, go ahead and give it your best shot. If it doesn't work, no big deal. At least you've learned that lesson." It helps kids if you keep failure in a healthy context: It's a normal, natural part of life. You might tell them about one of your own failures to show how it wasn't the end of the world for you.

Minor league baseball games are exciting to watch precisely because minor leaguers get ample chance to make mistakes. In fact, baseball players who are brought up too soon from the minor leagues rarely do well in the majors. Managers like to "season" them. That's why the idea of allowing your kids to fail at home is such a positive one. You want your child's mettle to be tested in the "minor leagues"—where she can feel comfortable finding the courage to risk, and know your encouragement to keep trying when she fails.

Way #5: Choose Your Words Carefully

Actress Gwyneth Paltrow has described herself as "the daddy's girl of all time."[4] Her father, Bruce Paltrow, took Gwyneth to Paris when she was 10 so that "she could see the city for the first time with a man who would always love her." Gwyneth remembers the way her father's words provided "a huge safety net" for her.

"My father had that incredible Jewish warmth," said Gwyneth, whose dad died a few days after her 30th birthday. She remembers him "really bolstering us [Paltrow and her brother] all the time. And when you're 9 years old and you're hearing that you are the best person, it gets in there, and you think, 'OK, I'm not going to be afraid to try things, because I'm always loved no matter what.'"[5]

Proverbs tells us that "the tongue has the power of life and death" (18:21). I see this truth played out in families across the country.

Everyone knows the saying "Sticks and stones may break my bones, but words will never hurt me." The truth is, words do have the power to tear down; some words, once said, are hard to take back. "Reckless words pierce like a sword," Proverbs warns (12:18), and a "scoundrel's" speech "is like a scorching fire" (16:27).

But words also have a miracle-working power: "The tongue of the wise brings healing" (Proverbs 12:18b). Speech that communicates positive expectations is a vital part of setting that home court advantage. Paltrow said her father "was the one person in your life that you always think, 'I'm safe because they're there, and they're so smart, and they know everything, and I can always go to them.'"[6]

Isn't this how you want your kids to think of you? The right words help your child see you as a safe place, someone who's always approachable and there for them.

"That kills me, when I think about it," Paltrow added. "It totally breaks my heart, how lucky I am."[7]

Way #6: Have the Conversation

No, I'm not talking about *that* conversation. Not the birds and bees. What I have in mind may be even more important.

At some point you need to have a conversation with your son or daughter in which you say something like, "No matter what you do in life, I'll always love you. You may be mean to your sister, you may not be nice to us, you may reject our faith, become a liar, a thief, or some combination of all of the above—but I will *always* love you. That will *never* change."

What's the point of that? you might ask. You might even think it better to strike a little fear in your child's heart by telling him to stay in line, or else.

Many kids rebel because they feel that all their parents care about is having kids who turn out according to their expectations. For those who believe in God, the message He gives us is that He loves us no matter what we do. We don't have to clean ourselves up to come to Him.

That's why the Bible's story of the prodigal son[8] is so powerful. No matter how deep that child got into trouble, floundering around in the muck of his mistakes, his father still loved him. Telling your child that you love him even if he doesn't meet all your positive expectations helps instill in him the desire to choose a good path.

Way #7: Give Them Ownership of the Family

I often arrive at hotels late and hungry enough to eat the lobby brochures. At that point, I'll even consider a restaurant that serves nothing but snack-size peanuts and soft drinks.

"Is your restaurant still open?" I'll ask the clerk.

"No, that closes at 10:00."

"How about room service?"

"The kitchen closed at 11:00."

I look at my watch; it's 11:03 P.M.

Now, if the manager of that hotel is smart, he or she will have empowered the person at the check-in desk to take charge of such situations. If a hotel hasn't done that, then I'll hear, "Sorry, there's nothing I can do about it."

But if the hotel manager is helping employees take ownership of the business and giving them freedom to make things happen, I'm more apt to hear, "Are you trying to find a full dinner?"

"No, ma'am. It's late. All I want is a sandwich."

"Well, let me see if I can talk to the cook before he leaves to put together a sandwich for you. Would that be okay?"

"That would be great."

Employees who care only for Number One aren't thinking about the business, but about hightailing it out of there and getting home before Jay Leno comes on. Empowered employees are thinking about the hotel's reputation, about helping those who come through its doors. They take ownership of their work.

In a similar way, you empower your children on the home court. You prepare kids a little at a time to give back to the family, to be responsible and accountable. Rather than keeping your kids on a leash and doing everything yourself, you let them take ownership of the family and home. To even try that, of course, you need positive expectations.

Kids who feel ownership will respect and give back to the family. When friends or extended family come over, children raised with a home court advantage do their part to pitch in and help. They recognize that home isn't a hotel in which the management (Dad and Mom) takes care of everything. In the "home court" family, not pitching in has consequences: loss of privileges to use the car, for instance, or to go out for the evening with friends.

Children with the home court advantage also recognize that their parents are not slave dogs that clean up after them, and that doing chores really does make a difference to the family. Kids can research movie show times, help plan the family camping trip, or map the vacation to see Grandma. The parent who delegates to instill a sense of ownership in her child is putting her positive expectations into action.

Most families are run autocratically; there's a king and a queen, and in a single-parent home usually it's a queen. With this kind of organizational chart it's easy to raise kids who don't care what happens to the castle because they don't own it. They become takers, expecting the benevolent despots to do all the giving.

When I worked as a dean of students at the University of Arizona, we decided to expect the best of kids. We made paint available for them to decorate their dorm rooms. We charged them a little, maybe $15, for the paint.

Did they graffiti their walls, or toss cans from the dorm rooftops to create modern art on the sidewalk? No. They painted their rooms and took much better care of the place because they'd invested in it.

That's the way it works with kids with the home court advantage. You don't expect them to be geniuses or even standouts; you just expect *their* best and give them a chance to display it, and forgive them when they don't.

So give them ownership, and expect them to do their part. More often than not, they will.

Let's Remember:

- Reflect on your own childhood and the resulting expectations you have for your children so that you don't saddle them with the same painful memories.
- If tension has built over the years between you and your child due to your expectations, don't let it leak into his adulthood. Address it now, but do so sensitively, making changes carefully and discussing them as needed over the coming months.
- There's something wonderfully freeing about having a normal, average kid who isn't pressured to be top student or starting quarterback.
- Positive expectation is full of grace; take failure in stride and don't make it a bigger deal than it is. Your child will get off center occasionally; the important thing is that he's going in the right direction and learning inner responsibility at home.
- Play on your child's team. That doesn't mean dropping everything for her; you're simply seeking to help meet her real, honest-to-goodness needs whenever you can.
- Your words matter; the "home court" parent has positive expectations and empowers her children through what she says.
- Have a conversation with your child in which you say something to the effect of, "No matter *what* you do in life, I will *always* love you. That will *never* change."

- Rather than keeping your kids on a leash and doing everything yourself, let them take ownership of the family and home. Prepare them a little at a time to give back to the family, to be responsible and accountable.

Back to School

A Homegrown Approach to an

Outside Education

few weeks after sending out acceptance and rejection letters for the Massachusetts Institute of Technology's Class of 2006, Marilee Jones, dean of admissions, received a curt reply from a disgruntled father. Written on the dad's corporate letterhead, it read, "You rejected my son. He's devastated. See you in court."

Ironically, Marilee received another letter the very next day—this one from the man's son. It read: "Thank you for not admitting me to MIT. This is the best day of my life."[1]

Many parents are desperate not only to get their child's foot in the door at a prestigious school, but to wrench that door off its hinges. "At MIT," said Jones, "we've been asked to return an application already in process so the parent can double-check his/her child's spelling. We've been sent daily faxes by parents with updates on their child's life. We've been asked by parents whether they should use their official letterhead when writing a letter of recommendation for their own child."[2]

By now you understand that raising your child with the home court advantage doesn't mean trying to railroad her into Harvard. It doesn't mean "fixing" his or her application, either. Parental overinvolvement in this area goes against the very grain of "home court" parenting. If I complete the college application, I'm teaching a sad but clear lesson: "It doesn't matter how you play the game; it matters only whether you win or lose. You and I both know this is as much my application as yours, but character and integrity aren't as important as you getting in."

You've essentially told your child lying is okay, and that you don't believe she has what it takes to make it on her own. I'd rather send my children to Podunk Community College to study window washing than send them to Yale with that philosophy ringing in their ears!

This attitude begins long before Junior or Missy goes off to college, of course. It starts way back in kindergarten.

School: Your First Proving Ground

Whether you homeschool or send your kids to a public or private school, your attitude toward school will be a major part of his educational experience.

School is usually a child's first proving ground outside the home—and a major benchmark for parents' expectations. It segregates children according to age (or at least grade level), then offers measures of performance based on below average, average, and above average. Whether this is wise isn't the point; it's what is done, and it tempts many parents to judge their own competence and identity according to how their children measure up.

I don't expect perfect grades from my kids. I'm more interested that they give it their best shot. That 4.0 with a garnish of extracurricular activities may get your child into an Ivy League school, but one day those grades will gather dust in boxes in the garage.

Some parents treat even preschool with cutthroat seriousness. Last time I checked, the "pre" in "preschool" meant "*before* school." Many parents go nuts because their kids didn't get into the "right" preschool. This kind of attitude places inordinate pressure on children to stand out academically. It tempts them to cut corners and value achievement over character.

The Pressure to Cheat

I walked into the kitchen one morning and found a piece of paper on the table on which Lauren had written:

> *Latin Test: Tuesday, May 20th*
> *Conjugate verbs (that means puts endings on them)*

Suddenly, the years melted away. I caught myself reciting:
laudo (I praise)
laudas (you praise)
laudat (he praises)
laudamus (we praise)
laudant (they praise)

Lauren's note revived many (painful) memories for me. It took me five tries to pass Latin; even then I only passed because Carl Maahs was kind enough to lower his left shoulder.

Cheating my way through Latin cost me in two senses: Not only did I fail to learn the material, but I also didn't acquire study skills like discipline, teamwork, and creative thinking (well, maybe I exercised a bit of creative thinking). Those skills—*character* skills—are a home-grown education's most important lessons.

Unfortunately, too many kids aren't learning those lessons. Aaron Eisman, a high school senior in an affluent Connecticut town, confessed that "in Westport, getting a B is like getting an F. So if you don't feel you can achieve it on your own, you find another way."[3] That "other way" for *three out of four* students these days includes cheating—from loading calculators with additional software to looking at a neighbor's test, as I did in Latin class.

Dr. Suniya S. Luthar, developmental psychologist at Teachers College at Columbia, studies affluent teenagers like the ones in Westport. In this group, which "she describes sympathetically as 'a truly miserable group of kids,'" she sees "higher rates of depression, anxiety, binge drinking and cheating . . . which she attributes to two causes: pressure to achieve and a lack of meaningful contact with adults."[4]

Lack of meaningful contact with adults. If that's not a cry for a family to focus on the home court, I don't know what is! Today's kids, driven to succeed from the day they dropped their diapers, need adults to step up to the plate and start stressing character and honesty over achievement with deception.

Grade the Grades

Occasionally I'm approached by a parent during a conference and asked, "What should I do about my child whose grades aren't that great?"

"What kind of a kid is she?" I'll ask.

"Oh, she's a great kid," the parent usually replies. "She's a caring sister," or, "He's a wonderful brother."

"Does your kid obey you?"

"Sure."

"Wow," I'll say, "you're blessed to have a kid like that."

"Well, Dr. Leman, we already knew that," the parent might respond, assuming I've missed the point of the question.

"Hear what I'm saying," I'll continue. "I'm telling you that your average 13-year-old makes a lot of choices in life. Today's teen is always within reach of drugs, sex, alcohol, shoplifting, vandalizing, you name it. Those things are all one easy step away. You must have done something right to raise a child that respects your values and thinks of others first. That says a lot more to me than whether their grade point average is 2.7 or 3.7."

Some parents have to stop and think. "Yeah," they may admit, "we really are blessed to have the kid we do."

"You have to grade the grades," I add.

"Huh? What does that mean?"

"It means you need to put the grades into perspective. Look at your kid's abilities, her level of dedication, her work ethic, and her life in general, and then grade the importance of her grades on that basis. I'd rather have a daughter who gets a B on a civics test and yet still sends thoughtful letters to her grandmother, than an obsessed student who gets an A+ in civics class but never talks to her grandparents because she thinks they're boring and they smell funny."

Am I lowering the bar too much by taking the focus away from grades? No. I hope we have realistic expectations that call our children to grow in their gifts and abilities—and to do the best they can in school. But I don't see grades as the primary problem among kids today. Putting those grades in perspective—that's the issue that needs attention.

Just think: When was the last time someone asked to see your middle school report card? How long has it been since someone asked for your high school transcripts? How many years have passed since anyone mentioned the college you graduated from (or didn't graduate from)?

I have to confess, I'm a guy who, when questioned by his mom about why he got one C and four F's on a mid-term report card, said, "I dunno. I guess I just concentrated too hard on one subject." But did my lack of early academic success keep me from doing what I do today? Not at all! In fact, it's given me a lot of funny material!

If your child is getting the kind of grades I got growing up, tell him or her, "I'm sorry to see that you don't like school." But is he learning? Does he like to take apart engines and find out what makes them work? Does she love to read Jane Austen novels on her own? Is he fascinated by movies, constantly borrowing your camcorder to direct his buddies in an amateur flick? I'm more concerned about whether my children are learning than I am about whether they're graduating in the top 10 or 20 percent of their class.

Likewise, when you see *good* grades on a report card, don't go playing college placement officer. Don't say, "We're so proud of you—the colleges will be knocking down our front door to get you to come to their school!" Say, "It's great to see that you enjoy learning. I'll bet you're proud of those grades." Or, "All that extra work you've done is really paying off!"

If your child is getting middle-of-the-road grades, and you honestly feel she's capable of doing better, ask what *she* thinks of her grades. She may admit she can do better. Then again, if she doesn't have the confidence to match her abilities, she may underestimate her potential.

This takes time. It's a homegrown approach that assumes you don't take a 13-year leave of absence as soon as your child enters kindergarten and expect "the professionals" to take over. You've got to know your child, know what she's learning, and know what the teacher is saying to make an evaluation. If you're running from the office to the Chinese take-out counter for dinner, then doing work on your laptop while you tuck the kids into bed, you won't have the inclination or peace of mind to do this.

Your child needs your involvement now more than ever. If he or she senses that you've pulled away, that your house has become a hotel instead of a home, the school years will be harder than they have to be.

Homework on the Home Court

You'll never hear me ask my kids, "Do you have homework?" They know whether they do, and my pesky reminders would only nag them to face something they should be facing themselves. Children who have grown up with the home court advantage take ownership of their homework; studying diligently is part of their responsibility.

I remember sitting down with one of our children and saying, "Honey, these are *your* grades. I don't know why they send them to our house with your mother's and my name on them, because they're yours, but they do. And in nine months, some stranger whom you've never met is going to look at an 8-by-11-inch piece of paper with your name, your address, and these grades, and make all sorts of assumptions about you. They don't know you like I know you; they don't see behind the figures. All they see is a name and a number. Now, understanding that, what do you think we should do about *your* grades?"

Your part is to help prepare a study area. Provide a desk and chair, and make sure the area is well lit. Let your child know that the desk isn't there for decorative purposes.

Many parents turn the living room into night school after the child has already done an hour of homework. I'm not willing to turn my family's life upside down for school. When kids bring work home, make sure there are limits to the amount of time they spend. The PTA and the National Educational Association recommend the ten-minute rule: Take your child's grade level and multiply it by ten, and that's generally a good limit on how many minutes she should be studying in the evening if homework is given (thirty minutes for a third grader, one hour for a sixth grader, etc.). If it takes more than that, there's a problem somewhere along the line.

But what if homework isn't getting done? Suppose you know that your eight-year-old son hasn't done his homework because you heard him in his room listening to the basketball game. Here's where reality discipline kicks in. You don't need to pester him 10 times, saying, "Jehoshaphat, why aren't you doing your homework? How many times have I told you this evening to turn off that radio?"

Instead, don't say anything. Secretly call the teacher in the morning before class and say, "Mrs. McGillicuddy, I was just calling to let you know that Jehoshaphat didn't do a lick of homework last night." Then the teacher can call him to the front of the classroom that morning and say, "Jehoshaphat, I was wondering if you would start off class by showing us the answers to our homework problems."

Have the teacher hold Jehoshaphat accountable for his actions. You'll need to know your child, of course, to assess whether this will provide an appropriate jolt to his priorities. But even little Jehoshaphat can—and should—be held accountable for his actions by reality discipline. The "reality" is that he's responsible for getting his homework done on time; the "discipline" is the teacher calling him on the carpet—literally. If this is a pattern in your child, the brief injury to his ego will cost less in the long run than habitual irresponsibility.

There's another way in which kids need to take ownership of their school experience. I'm talking about the job of communicating what's going on at school.

On the way home from school one afternoon, Lauren talked excitedly about a mosaic they were creating in her classroom. She explained the process of creating its layers, and how it would take a couple weeks to finish the whole thing. I'm not sure I understood it all. But that's why I'm a psychologist and not a mosaic artist.

I never ask my kids what they learned in school. Sooner or later they'll tell me about it, and it's healthier for them to initiate the conversation. Most young kids will tell you what they're thinking without you having to ask.

So don't ask a young child, "What did you do in school, honey?" Young kids will answer, though if you ask them about it habitually, you've usually beaten that out of them by about fourth grade. Once they feel that answering that question is "reporting in," you won't get more than "nuthin'." If we set up a system in which we do all the questioning, kids learn over time to give us rote responses.

One mom I talked to didn't understand this. I turned to her husband and asked, "When you've finished an eight-hour day at work, how eager are you to go over every little detail of it with your wife? How does that sound?"

"Terrible!" he confessed. "I want to relax at home. The last thing I want to do is relive the very thing I'm trying to escape from."

"That's exactly my point!" I said. "Let your son's home be a home, a place of refuge, a place where he can recover from the stresses of school rather than being forced to relive them."

Backwards to the Future

In a society that pushes kids forward, parents who set a home court advantage tend to let their children find their own pace. That's certainly true when it comes to education.

If your child isn't quite getting the coursework, she doesn't seem to be as emotionally and socially mature as her classmates, and you're getting signals from the teacher to consider holding her back, don't get defensive. Don't yell, "Why do you say that about my daughter? She's very bright!"

No doubt she is. But intelligence and readiness are two different things. It doesn't take a Ph.D. in psychology to realize that children mature at different rates. Unfortunately, most parents latch on to their child's school status as if his or her life depended on it.

Don't get me wrong. Just because I topped out in school with D's, I'm not advocating a lower standard. But don't push your kids into the next grade if they aren't getting the material. If you're in doubt, hold them back. And if your child's teacher is in doubt, hold back on making a quick judgment.

It may seem traumatic now, but I guarantee that whether a boy or girl graduated from high school at 18 or 19 won't mean *anything* 10 or even 2 years down the road. Can you imagine a company saying, "Well, we'd really like to promote Stan instead of Alice; he's better with people, more at ease with administration, and seems to have a better grasp of our company's business. But Alice was only 16 when she graduated from high school and Stan was 19. I guess we'll have to go with Alice."

That conversation will never happen. But let's say Stan's parents decided to push him through school, even though he wasn't making it. Here's one conversation that might happen: "Stan seems to have the mind for this job, but he just doesn't have the confidence. And socially, I'm not sure he has what it takes to command others' respect. For that reason, I think Alice has the edge for this new position."

Your child's future employers will look at his or her character, social skills, and other abilities. They won't think to question how long it took your child to get out of high school. All they'll care about is the *quality* of the person who emerged.

Lauren, our youngest, was barely out of the starting blocks in school when we fired the gun again to start her over in kindergarten. Did holding her back a year mean that she was destined to forever lag behind? No. Did it damage her psyche because of a perceived failure? Hardly. Parents who read that into the situation are the ones who could make a negative impact in their child's life due to hovering hypervigilance.

Today, Lauren is brighter than bright. She can literally recite the Latin alphabet forward and backward, and spell almost anything in English that comes her way.

If you have siblings close in age, though, questions may be popping up in your mind. What happens when you have one child a year younger than the first? Are you going to hold your firstborn back a year, putting both children in the same grade? That's not a good idea, because you want to keep kids apart as much as possible.

If you have a child born in November, for example, and a second child born fifteen months later in February, make your decision with all kids in mind—and the more separation between the kids the better. If that firstborn November child is a little bluebird and your second-born February child is noticeably slow, you might put the firstborn in with kids his own age and then hold the second back a year. The gap would then be two years between them, which would help that second-born in particular. What you *wouldn't* want to do is push that slower developing second-born into the wake of that brainy little firstborn.

Getting the Teacher on Your Side

Having a "home court" philosophy means getting involved—in this case, working with your child's teachers.

Maybe you can recite the introductory speech from PTA meetings and open houses. They say the same thing every year: "It's so nice to see parents here this evening working hand in hand with the school to broaden the horizons of the next generation."

The fact is, parents and teachers *don't* always work well together, and often are at odds with one another. But when you feel the urge to take sides against your child's teacher, give that teacher the benefit of the doubt. If you hear from your child that the teacher did this or said that, don't call the principal—*call the teacher*. Go directly to the source.

Say, "Listen, I got this from a nine-year-old, but I want to get it from you. Here's what I heard happened in class today, but I wanted your take on it." Not only do you get "the rest of the story," but your child learns that she can't mealy-mouth her way out of a situation by blaming someone else.

Having two children and a son-in-law who've worked in education, I've seen the system from all sides. It's natural for teachers to have a particular affinity for some students over others. We're all human; there are some personality types we get along with, and some we don't. But instead of making wild accusations of favoritism, try to understand what's getting in the way of your child and teacher having a productive relationship. Help the teacher understand your unique child.

This could be a valuable learning experience for your son or daughter, too. You might say something like this: "Honey, it's obvious that you and your teacher don't get along all that well. But I've spoken with him, and I believe he'll grade you fairly. You know, in one sense, this is a great opportunity to prepare you for the future. The day is going to come when you have a boss you might not get along with all that well, either—but you're going to have to learn how to work in that person's company anyway, just like today you have to learn how to be a student in this teacher's classroom."

Your child's teacher may have as few as 20 students or as many as 100. It's not fair to expect him or her to immediately understand the best way to work with a kid that you've known and loved for years. Get on your teacher's side, work with her, and your child will benefit.

When "Home Court" Becomes Homeschooled

Seventeen-year-old Aaron Brown, a high school student from Arlington, Texas, has been homeschooled most of his life, but recently he returned to school.[5] Not traditional public or private school, but something between those options and homeschooling.

Brown attends Grace Preparatory School,[6] where he spends about 15-20 hours each week in the classroom, or roughly half the time that traditional public or private high school students do. The rest of his free time must be used for scheduling his own homework and study, which is exactly what will be expected of him in college.

This approach, known as university-model schooling (UMS), is a growing alternative to traditional public and private schooling, as well as homeschooling—and reflects the strengths of both.

In traditional public school, students typically spend 35-40 hours per week in the classroom; homeschoolers, on the other hand, spend few, if any, hours in a formal classroom setting. When the traditional student and the homeschooled student enter college and are expected to spend about 15 credit hours per week in class and many more outside class, the transition requires significant adjustment—especially if the inner trait of discipline hasn't been adequately developed.

UMS draws on the strength of traditional schooling in its preparation for college's structured classroom experience—plus the parental involvement and encouragement of self-discipline that are hallmarks of homeschooling. It closely tracks with the aim of nurturing children from the inside out.

During early UMS elementary school classes, parents are highly involved in instruction. They move gradually from the role of tutor to course monitor in the secondary school years, when the number of classroom hours increases.

Like the homeschool model, UMS fosters character development and helps children grow in independence, while still allowing a high degree of parent-child interaction—your indelible imprint—along the way. I endorse UMS wholeheartedly for families looking for an option between traditional public/private schooling and homeschooling.

In case you hadn't noticed, there's a similarity between children with a home court advantage and homeschooled children: parental nurture that grows maturity. "In 1992 psychotherapist Larry Shyers did a study while at the University of Florida in which he closely examined the behavior of 35 home schoolers and 35 public schoolers. He found that home schoolers were generally more patient and less competitive. They tended to introduce themselves to one another more; they didn't fight as much. And the home schoolers were much more prone to exchange addresses and phone numbers. In short, they behaved like miniature adults."[7]

It's not my intention to advocate homeschooling over public schooling or other methods of private schooling. All have their merits and disadvantages. I simply want you to note a strength shared by homeschooled and "home court" children: When a parent serves as the child's primary teacher, in school or in life, that parent has more influence. The child has a deeper understanding of who Mom and Dad are; the interaction generally fosters deeper friendships between parent and child, and an appreciation for the family's values.

Some critics of homeschooling warn that homeschoolers may not be "socialized" properly. I haven't found this to be a powerful argument. For starters, only in school are we segregated according to age. I've found homeschooled kids to be very adept at getting along with older children, younger children, and adults. They tend to be less "cliquish" and more mature in a variety of social settings.

Homeschoolers may also be less likely to get overly interested in the opposite sex at too young an age. When a child feels secure at home, he or she may not crave emotional validation that comes from outside. It's uncommon to see homeschoolers pairing off in elementary or middle school—and that's a big plus in my book. Even middle schoolers are too young to form intense, emotionally involved, exclusive relationships with the opposite sex.

Having said all this, let me state that our children weren't homeschooled. They had some wonderful teachers, and we're thrilled with the experience they've had educationally. That's why I don't advocate one choice over another.

For some families, homeschooling may not be the best option. But I did want to point out the connection between the homeschool and "home court" philosophies: The family should be the center of your child's emotional world.

You, the parent, should be your child's biggest influence and greatest inspiration. Rooting your children's identity in your home and family is vital when facing the proving ground of school.

Let's Remember:

- School is usually a child's first proving ground outside the home, and a major litmus test for parents' expectations. Try to keep your parental ego out of it.

- Ask yourself: Are you more concerned about whether your children are learning, or whether they're graduating in the top 10 percent of their class?

- Don't turn your home into night school in an effort to push your children.

- If your child is getting middle-of-the-road grades, and you honestly feel she's capable of doing better, ask her what *she* thinks of her grades.

- Nurture inner responsibility by avoiding the question, "Do you have homework?" with your child. Don't ask young children, "What did you learn in school today?" Sooner or later, they'll tell you about it—and it's healthier for them to initiate the conversation.

- Children mature at different rates. Many parents latch on to their child's test scores and class placement stats as if the kid's life depended on it. It doesn't.

- Whether you use the homeschool, public school, private school, or university-model school, make an indelible imprint on your child by rooting his identity in your home and family.

Balancing Work and Family

I n spite of exhaustion and a nagging cold, Mark managed to make it to his church's weekend men's conference. Late Saturday night, Stan, a man Mark respected, approached him.

"Can I be honest with you?" Stan asked.

"Sure," Mark replied.

"Mark," he said, "I see you as a guy who's strung out. You want to do everything well, and you're *trying* to do everything. But you can't; you'll burn out. How many hours per week do you work?"

"Probably 55 to 65," Mark replied.

"You need to cut it to 40," Stan said.

"Stan," Mark protested, "I don't know *anyone* who works 40 hours."

Stan, who owned his own company, replied, "Well, I don't know anyone who *doesn't* work 40. You just make it happen. Has Shelly ever talked to you about this?"

"Yeah, of course."

"Don't wait until you're as old as I am to listen to your wife," said Stan. "God gives us our wives for a reason."

Later Mark reflected, "When he had that conversation with me, it snapped me to attention. There were a few things converging in my life: that conversation, talking with Shelly back at home, and a sermon I heard called 'Choosing to Cheat' by Andy Stanley, which pointed out our lack of time to get everything done that we want. All of us have to 'cheat' someone out of the time we'd like to spend on them, and we tend to give our best to work or our hobbies, and cheat our family, who gets the leftovers."

Even after Mark and Shelly decided he would cut back, Mark didn't know if he could pull it off. "I had just turned in an aggressive budget for my work," he said. "If you're working 60 hours and you suddenly cut back to 40, you're essentially cutting a part-time person from your office. But Stan pep-talked me enough, and Shelly and I followed through with the decision. In the end, we believed he was right."

You can't maintain the home court advantage if you're never at home. I know, I know—if you don't work, you can't afford to *buy* a home, not to mention feed and clothe your family. But when your job overwhelms your family life, you've allowed the means to drown the end.

It's time to get back on top of the water, my friend.

We Mean Business

Sometimes when I'm on the road thousands of miles from home, settling into my hotel for the weekend before speaking at a conference, I'll imagine what Sande and the kids are doing back in Tucson. I think, *What on earth am I doing here away from my family?*

After all, extensive travel doesn't seem to mix very well with maintaining a home court advantage. But the answer follows as sure as our family's next bill in the mailbox: *I'm making a living for my family.*

We might like to spend all our waking hours reading books with our kids, playing catch in the backyard, or going for family bike rides. But even though food grows on trees, the money to buy it doesn't. Unless your last name is Vanderbilt, Carnegie, or Rockefeller, you must earn a living for your family; supporting it both financially and emotionally can begin to feel like a circus juggling act.

Balancing these responsibilities is especially difficult in our overworked culture. The average American employee now works nearly 2,000 hours per year, which is over 300 hours more than French workers, 400 hours more than German workers, and 600 hours more than Norwegian workers. In every other industrial nation, the average number of hours worked per week is going down; only in developing nations such as Malaysia, Sri Lanka, and Thailand are the annual figures climbing along with those in the United States.[1]

For some companies, and some working parents, a kid is simply another ball in the air to juggle. But if we're to have kids who benefit from a home court advantage, our work must exist to support our families—not the other way around.

No Job Is That Important

As trusted advisor to President George W. Bush, Karen Hughes was arguably one of the most powerful women in America. Mark McKinnon, Bush's media adviser, estimated that President Bush turned to Hughes for 20 of the 100 big decisions he had to make every day. "He trusts her completely. He trusts her like he trusts no one."[2]

But Hughes put her family first. She decided in spring 2002 to step down from her position so that she and her family could return to Texas—a choice that surely seemed madness to many.

One night late that March, Karen and husband, Jerry, and son, Robert, gathered around their kitchen table. "I really think we all want to go home to Texas," she said. In hindsight she would admit, "It was a relief for me to finally say it out loud."

On April 17, following a meeting, Hughes asked Chief of Staff Andrew Card to go on without her. She had something to talk about with the president, who was getting ready to walk the dogs.

"Mr. President," she said when the two of them were alone, "I love you, but my family and I want to go back to Texas." They continued walking out of the White House and onto the manicured grounds as the president took in the stunning news.

"I know your family is a priority," he replied, "always have."[3]

No matter what your job, having homegrown children means putting family relationships first. You may feel indispensable to your work, and colleagues may heap affirmation on you—affirmation you may not get at home. But there's no business more important than family.

Don't Give It Your All

How often do you or your spouse get home from work, having "given your all," with nothing left for your family? If we had annual performance reviews at home, many of us might be fired from our parenting responsibilities for failure to do our duty at home.

I suggest that breadwinners don't give their all to their work. If you pour 110 percent of your time and energy into pushing papers or training mechanics, what's left at home for pushing your kid on the swing and training your daughter to be a loving sister? If you give *everything* to your work, you won't have the emotional and physical resources to give your family what it needs.

It's not like this world always rewards those who give their all at work, anyway. Former Kansas City Chief's head coach Gunther Cunningham was so dedicated to his job that the day after the season ended he was still in his office at five in the morning—even though it was *Christmas Day.*

His reward?

He was fired two weeks later.

In my travels I've heard many heartbreaking tales of eager young women and men who put in long hours to make partner, get the corner office, become a V.P., you name it—only to be dumped when someone who's willing to stay a little longer or play office politics a little better comes along. And what about those who fall victim to mergers, reorganizations, or downsizing?

Life is short, and kids are kids for such a short time. As much as I love my work, I want to be there for my kids' activities; I don't want to miss their special events, even if it means sitting on an emptier wallet or waking up in a smaller house.

How do you avoid giving your all to work? First, make quitting time as absolute as starting time. You wouldn't show up for work an hour late; don't show up for home "late" either.

Second, leave your work at work. If you must take work home, resolve to do it only after the last child is in bed and your spouse is occupied with something else. You gave at least eight or nine hours to the office already; your family deserves your full attention for at least half that time.

Third, if your job is so stressful that you can't keep a decent schedule or avoid coming home wiped out, *get another job.*

"But it's not that easy!" you might say.

I never said it was. But your family's success is worth a good, hard effort, isn't it?

If your work is too demanding, find other work. That's putting it bluntly, and it may sound drastic. But what's the alternative? Well-fed, well-clothed, well-educated kids you never relate to?

Some organizations also ask employees to sacrifice by relocating. If yours asks you to move from Sante Fe to Seattle, and your extended family and friends are in Sante Fe, my vote is that you stay in Santa Fe at all reasonable costs. If you move to Seattle, you surrender a benefit no amount of money can compensate for: the relationships of grandparents, other relatives, and established friends. A healthy extended family is a lot to toss out the window for a few extra bucks and a new title on your business card.

Your priorities pave the way for your decisions—so get them straight. If your work exists to support your family, you'll be more apt to leave the office while others work late, and forgo promotions in favor of time together as a family. You'll tend to see work as a means, not an end.

I know from experience that it's hard to sit in a hotel room watching the Weather Channel when you'd rather be home watching the thunder and lightning storm with your kids over popcorn, comforting your little one, and oohing and aahing with the older ones. When you can't help being on the road, use phone calls to keep bedtime routines intact, saying prayers or singing cherished songs together. Some traveling parents even record a reading of a child's favorite book so that he or she can listen to the tape while they're away. It isn't the same as being there in person, of course, but shows your love—and makes the reunion at home that much sweeter.

Buy a Ticket to Your Child's Life

Lauren told me on the phone, long-distance, that she was going to sing a solo in the school concert. I could tell from the excitement in her voice that she really wanted me to be there for her moment of glory.

So I wiggled out of all kinds of work obligations and hurried home from a trip so I could see her perform. It cost me a king's ransom to be there—nearly $10,000.

Arriving just in time, I walked into the school auditorium—expecting to see rows of squirming, jabbering kids. But no one was there.

Had I gotten the time wrong?

I hustled to the school office. "What happened to the school concert?" I asked.

"What concert?" the woman replied. "We don't know of any school concert. Why don't you check your daughter's classroom?"

I set off down the hallway. Reaching Lauren's second grade room, I entered—just as my daughter delivered her six-word solo in a little class play.

That was the "concert." The cost of getting there made for the highest priced ticket I've ever bought for any event—but I was there!

You know what? It was worth it. When I saw Lauren's face light up as I walked into the room, I realized I hadn't just bought an expensive plane ticket—I'd purchased a memory with my daughter that may last a lifetime. Even if she forgets this event—though I doubt she will—she'll still know that when it really mattered, I was there.

I hear business moguls talk all the time about marketing their products. Well, how about marketing our love to our kids? While Madison Avenue seeks to sell them jeans, perfume, and the latest CD, let's advertise our interest, our commitment, and our involvement.

In business terms, that's what I was doing: marketing my concern and my devotion to Lauren. The money I spent on my "marketing campaign" could have purchased a full-page ad in our local newspaper, but this wasn't a one-day sale. It was a lifetime memory. I wasn't peddling a better mousetrap; I was proclaiming my love and commitment to my precious little daughter.

I know guys who drop 400 bucks to buy the latest titanium driver, and all that does is put their little white golf ball a few yards further out of bounds! Yet those same dads balk at the thought of parting with half that much money to be at an important event in their children's lives.

Make no mistake: There are costs to pay when balancing work and family. Some parents will refuse higher paying promotions because the time and travel would take too much. Others will go to work earlier so they can return home before their kids get back from school. Still others will sacrifice years of work or give up their careers altogether to focus on their children.

I'm not pretending the cost isn't real or significant. I'm admitting that, *yes*, parenting will ask you to sacrifice. I'm a realist! As a working dad, I live with this reality every day.

But I'm also saying the costs and sacrifice are worth it. They're the absolute best investment you can make.

The Homestretch Home

If you're going to sacrifice in order to gain family time, you may as well make it quality time. That means making the transition from workday to home in a way that doesn't leave you wrung out.

Not every commute home from work is filled with relaxing thoughts and a deep reservoir of energy to give kids. I know what that feels like.

You've had a hectic day. As you drive through traffic, you need a restroom like you've never needed anything else. For the last seven miles, you've even considered making use of the empty pop bottle one of your kids left in the car, but you figure you can make it to your house.

When this happens, call your spouse on the cell phone and say, "Honey, I'm five minutes away, but when I get there I really need to go potty. I'm about to bust a bladder. Just give me three minutes." Win the pledge of your mate and kids not to pounce on you right away.

Next, prepare your mind. Maybe you love listening to political discussions heating up talk radio on the drive home, or keeping in touch with Wall Street's ups and downs at the market's close. But choose a different station, something that soothes you, like soft elevator music or oldies.

Maybe when you get home you love to check the mail and peruse the newspaper. Decide instead not to go through either right away. (To keep a future visit to the urologist at bay, however, accept that when you get home, you really *should* go potty.)

Finally, realize that, although you're exhausted, the kids have been home for a few hours and they probably want a little piece of you. If you're smart, you'll give it to them.

Maintaining that home court advantage for your kids means communicating, *I love you more than this briefcase, more than that newspaper sitting on the coffee table, and certainly more than that stack of bills sitting on the counter.* Those first seconds as you walk through the door (or after your potty break) set the tone of your time with your children.

Imagine what a gift it is when you demonstrate the message, *I'm so happy to see you!*

Taking That Step

Remember Mark from the beginning of the chapter? His 55 to 60 hours each week at the office were taking their toll on his energy and ability to be present with his wife and two kids. "It wasn't just a lack of time," he said. "I was wiped out when I got home."

After talking with Stan, Mark approached his boss as they walked out of a meeting.

"I just want you to know I'm cutting back on my hours," Mark said. "I'm not going to work 60 hours a week anymore. I'm not sure what's going to happen to my numbers and profitability, but it's what I have to do."

"Well," his boss replied, "there are times when you have to work those kind of hours."

"I understand that there *are* those times," Mark replied, "but I'm not going to do it anymore."

Mark and Shelly waited to see what would happen.

Not only did the office end up making its budget—it won awards for its work besides!

"The turnaround was amazing when I had more time and energy for my family," Mark said later. "I also have a lot more to give Shelly. We felt this was God saying, 'I take care of things when you make wise decisions.'"

Many people think the "home court" philosophy calls us to great sacrifice. In one sense, that's true. But in another sense, it provides the most stable foundation on which you can build your life—and often results in rewards that are bigger than anything you gave up.

God knows what He's talking about when He says you can do more working six days a week than you can in seven. Many women and men have found they can do much more working 40 hours a week and getting their batteries recharged at home than they can putting in 60-hour weeks and being depressed, anxious, and tired.

Why not give it a shot? For one month, put your family first. My guess is that you'll see the benefits—and you'll never want to go back to anything else.

Let's Remember:

- You may *feel* "indispensable" to your work, but you *are* indispensable to your family. Don't give your all at work; save time and energy for your kids.
- Choose your work commitments wisely. If you're asked to relocate, stay if at all possible—especially if you'd be leaving extended family. If your work is too demanding, find a different job.
- Advertise your interest, commitment, and love to your kids by spending time with them—even if it costs you money.
- Use your commute home from work to prepare yourself to spend quality time with your family.

Kiddie Kennel Kids

Larry King was interviewing Dr. Brenda Hunter, author of the book *Home by Choice: Raising Emotionally Secure Children in an Insecure World.* At the time, King was facing the birth of another child.

"Dr. Hunter," he asked, "does it really matter whose arms hold the child?"

Her answer, well researched in her book, was a definitive *yes.*

It does matter whose arms are holding the child. As that old song reminds us, the arms are connected to the shoulder bone; the shoulder bone's connected to the neck bone; the neck bone's connected to the head bone. And the head bone surrounds the brain—which is the center of your value system.

If you drop off your bleary-eyed two-year-old at day care around 6:30 A.M., pick him up at 6:30 P.M., and he goes to bed two hours later, who's teaching your child about life? Is it someone who's getting paid just above minimum wage, who two months ago decided to work at a day care center because she grew bored with folding clothes in the women's department of a store at the mall?

In institutional day care, your child may acquire the academic and social skills to "make the grade." But is that all you want from the new life you've introduced into the world? What good does it do me to have a child reading when he's three years old if he never calls home when he's thirty? Is that a good trade?

What's the Difference?

Let's be honest. Do you want a homegrown child, loyal to her family? Or do you want an institutionally grown child, who may be bitter over being raised by strangers whose names she can't recall, people she'll never see again?

If you want to believe that parents don't matter, that your child will grow up to be the same child whether he's at home, in day care, or raised by a pack of wolves—good luck. Your child's values and character are not determined solely by his genes. You may find research that claims there is no difference between preschool-aged children who stay at home and those who go to child care,[1] but in your heart of hearts, you know better.

Do you really need a $500,000 government study to understand that, of all the billions of people in the world, *you* are the one who makes the most difference in your child's life? Do you really need a Harvard professor to spell out in an academic journal that spending time with your children is good for them? Why even ask how much we can get away with being absent from our children's lives, when we all know the answer is *as little as possible*?

"I was once on the old Donahue show," said Dr. Laura Schlessinger, "being interviewed by him about [my book] *Ten Stupid Things Women Do to Mess Up Their Lives,* and even though there was nothing in there about daycare, they had, according to an audience member, stocked the audience with young feminist females to attack me, to make it controversial, to make it an interesting show. I was unaware at this time that TV was so phony. It was interesting because I got pretty irritated with the audience after a while and I said, 'OK, tell you what, if you could die and be recycled and come back as an infant, stand up if you would rather be raised by a daycare worker, a nanny, or a babysitter. Stand up now.'

"And, you know, in this whole audience that was attacking me like crazy, nobody stood up. The camera panned back—I have a tape of this, because every now and then I like to watch it—and nobody moved. So I said, 'Then why are you going to do this to your children?'"[2]

Most of us don't want anyone but our parents raising us. Yet many of us want to assuage our guilt for handing our kids over to day care. The blunt truth is that we can't have it both ways. If you want your children to receive maximum benefit from the home court advantage, child care outside the home is simply not the best option.

You may have heard of a recent study by the National Institute of Child Health and Human Development's (NICHD) Early Child Care Research Network. One of its most publicized findings: As children ages three months to four years spent more hours in nonmaternal child care (anyone except the mother), their levels of disobedience and aggression in kindergarten escalated, according to their teachers.

Some will point out that these behaviors were within normal ranges, meaning they weren't serious enough to require intervention. I believe, however, that the point still stands: Institutional day care is not as good a choice as full-time care by the child's mother or father.

Another study found that stress levels in toddlers (aged 16 to 38 months) increased over the course of a day at a day care center—especially when compared to infants. On days at home, stress levels decreased as the day progressed.[3]

What Are Your Options?

Most companies today will grant you a few months of maternity leave and a month or so of paternity leave. But they generally expect you to find a day care center or nanny and punch back in to work well before your baby has blessed you with her first laugh.

Because you fear losing your job or the career momentum you had before the baby arrived, you cut a few corners. "After all," you tell yourself, "she sleeps half the day anyway. It's not like I'm really gone from her for ten hours—she's sleeping three or four of them so those don't count!" You return to work a few days early, just to show your boss you're a "team player."

This can produce what I call Kiddie Kennel Kids—children who spend almost all their waking hours in day care throughout their preschool years. They're dropped off at 6:30 A.M. on the way to work and picked up at 6:30 P.M. on the way home. They'll grow up not knowing anything different.

If this is true of your child, I want to ask you something: Are you doing this for your child's benefit, or for yours?

I realize that you may not have the option of staying home, especially if you're a single parent. If you're doing it because you think preschool is a must, though, please think again. Preschool is all right as long as it's not overdone, but it certainly isn't necessary. I didn't go. Has that stopped you from reading this book? Is there a disclaimer on the cover that says, "By the way, Dr. Leman didn't go to preschool when he was three years old"?

If you've determined that preschool is best for your child, a three-year-old usually can handle two and a half hours a day, three times a week. But no two-year-old belongs in preschool. There's no "schooling" going on there; it's just babysitting by another name.

If, after reviewing your options, you decide that someone else must watch your child, consider a babysitting co-op. It has at least three advantages: Its cost is negligible or nonexistent; it allows your child to receive some of the socialization that can be a strength of preschools and day care centers; and, when it's your turn to help with the co-op, it lets you see your child interacting with other children.

If you're organizing the co-op yourself, you can choose those who are involved—making for shared values. The low cost may free up money in your budget, allowing you to remain home for more hours. And the quality of care and concern is likely to be higher.

Tough Questions

Where does this leave you if you're a single parent?

Most single mothers don't have the luxury of staying home without working. If you can use family day care or a child care co-op instead of institutional day care, by all means do it. Those options provide a higher degree of family interaction with those who already love your child.

For others, institutional child care may be necessary. If your child is at a day care facility, ask yourself these questions:

- Would you want to be there?
- Is it clean?
- Can you show up at any time?
- How do the teachers interact with the children?
- Does the program align with your values?

I know it's not popular to suggest that some people, in their present circumstances, are not able to give their children what's best for them. It's not my intention to add insult to injury. Do the best you can with what you have, making changes as you're able, with the goal of spending as much time with your kids as possible.

Whether or not you're a single parent, consider how your kids will someday view the child care choices you make today. In time, most children will come to appreciate your efforts to do the best you could with what you had; they'll have difficulty, however, if you *chose* to make work a priority over relationship.

All your son or daughter will know is how much time, effort, and sacrifice you seemed to make for his or her sake. I've sat in too many counseling rooms not to know that your kids will see time spent in day care as *their* sacrifice, not yours. You may think you're working extra hours for them, but they won't see it that way.

On the other hand, I've never had a kid resent the fact that one of his parents stayed home. Children always view that as a great gift and a clear sign of their parents' commitment to them.

The First Six Years

One of the most common questions I get on the road is this: "Dr. Leman, I'd really like to return to my job, but I don't want to short-change my child. How long should a mother stay at home before going back to work if she really wants to put her child's development first?"

I'll make sure we're talking turkey here and ask the mom if she really wants to know. "Are you asking me what is truly best for your child?"

"Yes," she'll say, expecting me to say something shocking—like six months.

"Then I recommend you stay home the first six *years* of your child's life. You may consider that a tall order, but when you think about it against the sweep of your life, it isn't much more than taking time off for college. Eighty percent of your child's personality is formed by age four, so if you can remain home during those formative years, so much the better. By age six, your child is starting school and the transition back to work—if you choose to return—will be a natural one."

"But no company will hold my job that long!" the woman might protest.

"I realize that, but that's not what you asked me. You asked me what was truly best for your child, and that's the question I answered. I believe every child deserves a full-time mom for the first six years of her life."

Is It Flex Time Yet?

Thankfully, there are all sorts of arrangements some companies have embraced to accommodate families—like sequencing, job sharing, part-time work, telecommuting, and flex scheduling.

I talk with a lot of flight attendants in my travels, and some have arrangements with the airline that allow them to work only a couple of days every couple weeks. These attendants figure they can find quality care—Grandma, a sister, or a close friend who's also a mom—for their kids during those two days, and they still get to keep their jobs and reduced-cost flight privileges to visit other family members.

If you call my office, you'll find that the hours are 7:00 A.M. to 3:00 P.M. Why? Because my assistant has a 16-year-old daughter. The "inconvenience" to an organization that wants to reach me at 4:00 P.M. doesn't matter half as much to me as the inconvenience to an adolescent who'd otherwise come home from school to an empty house.

Some families who strive for the home court advantage make other choices for the sake of their kids. They may move closer to work to create a shorter commute, downsize their monthly rent or mortgage, or even take a cut in pay.

If you have dominion over your schedule, you're in a good position to make changes. If you don't have that control, your time at home is particularly important. How are you going to spend it?

Are you doing the best right now with the time and money you have? If you're still deciding whether to work outside the home, make sure you have all the facts.

Count the Cost

If you're considering going back to work—or are currently working and want to reconsider staying at home—do the following first:

1. Ask yourself, *What am I working for? Why do I do what I do?* You may have multiple reasons, but if few of your motivations include family, that may indicate that work has a greater hold on you than it should.

2. Calculate how much returning to work will add to your income. Don't forget to subtract the cost of child care, taxes, clothes you'll need to buy for work, meals out, transportation to and from work (with perhaps the cost of using an extra car), house cleaning, etc.

Do the math. Is returning to work worth it? One source says you need to earn at least two and a half times the amount you pay for child care to make going back to work economically worthwhile.[4] Often a better option is to cut back on your expenses rather than send another parent to work to maintain your current lifestyle. A sacrifice here in terms of where or how you live may spell the difference between one parent and both parents working.

3. Ask yourself, *How long do I need to stick to the plan to stay at home?* We're not talking about tightening your belt for the rest of your life. Tight budgeting for a little longer than it takes to get a college degree is well worth it to have homegrown children. Of course, if you have *three* children, that college degree could become a Ph.D. Even so,

10 years still represents a fraction of an adult's life—but more than half of your child's.

4. Explore work-from-home alternatives or split scheduling. If you truly must work, try to find something that allows you to have at least one parent home whenever the kids are out of school (but make sure the two of you have sufficient time together so that you can maintain your marriage). Take a part-time job during school hours, even if the pay is less.

5. Finally, be brave enough to ask your son or daughter about your decision to return to work. Shoot straight. Ask her, "Honey, what do you think about Mommy going back to work?" Your child's response just might help with your decision.

Every Mom Is a Working Mom

"You were slated to become the first female black astronaut, yet you gave it up," host Sally Jessy Raphael challenged Helen Jackson on her daytime talk show. "Why?"

"My oldest son was having trouble in school," replied Helen, who had returned to work when Malik was three weeks old. "He was severely withdrawn and depressed. He had failed sixth grade. My son was fast becoming a statistic."[5]

You may have seen the bumper sticker that reads, "Every mother is a working mother." It's true. Whether or not a mother works outside the home following the birth of her child, she's got plenty of work to do.

But in recent years that truth hasn't gotten much respect. In one 1997 study, roughly 50 percent of adults said it was better for mothers to stay at home with their kids—down from 70 percent in 1977.[6] As I pointed out earlier, "72 percent of women with children under 18 are in the work force."[7]

There's been a recent positive trend, however: "55 percent of mothers with babies work outside the home, down from 59 percent in 1998. That's the first decrease since tracking began in 1976."[8]

I hope that indicates we're reaching a turning point, in which mothers opt out of corporate America. Many already have, or have chosen to work part-time instead of full-time. Having Mom at home is particularly important; consider that the already mentioned results of the NICHD's Early Child Care Research Network study hinged on the *mother's* involvement with the child.

To opt out, however, a mother needs options. Unfortunately, many families' lifestyles create a demand that can't be met unless both parents work outside the home. If possible, don't let finances dictate your decision.

"So Helen [Jackson] came home and began homeschooling her three older children," wrote Dr. Brenda Hunter. "After only nine months of homeschooling, all three children had soared by two or more grade levels in all academic areas. Malik, who had previously performed at the fourth grade level, now tested at the ninth grade level. No longer withdrawn and depressed, he began to develop socially and in time became a leader among his friends at church."[9]

"I'm not sorry that I gave up my career," Helen added. "Sure, I was doing my thing, but my kids were suffering. And I could never feel good if my children were unhappy."[10]

Instead of exploring space, Helen set out to explore her children's potential—a decision she *and* her children will no doubt look back on with gratitude.

Fathers: Wired to Nurture

"One of my first memories growing up was wishing my father would be home more," recalls Dr. Andrew Hudnut, a family physician in

Sacramento, California. "I was 8, and we had just returned from a canoe trip. I remember thinking, 'I don't want a bigger house or more money. I just want my dad around.' "[11]

Thankfully, more and more fathers are willing to sacrifice to gain that home court advantage with their children. "In a 2000 national survey, developed by the Radcliffe Public Policy Center at Harvard, 82 percent of men in their 20s and 30s said that things like salary and prestige aren't as important in a job as whether it'll allow them time with their family. . . . Increasingly, employers appear to be listening. Three in four businesses . . . surveyed by consulting firm Hewitt Associates said they offer such alternatives as part-time, flextime, job sharing, telecommuting, or a compressed week of longer workdays swapped for a day off. That's a 45 percent jump since 1990."[12]

Fathers' drive to return to the nest and nurture isn't only emotional. Research shows that in the weeks around the birth of a child, fathers show higher levels of estrogen and a rise in prolactin, the hormone that aids in lactation for women. There's also a 33 percent decrease in testosterone the first three weeks after the birth.[13] Why? The best guess is that "women's hormone levels are timed to the birth—and men's hormone levels are tied to their partners," says psychologist Anne Storey.[14]

Which means, Dad, that the stirrings to have homegrown children are wired into your nature from the moment your child arrives.

So are yours, Mom.

Listen to them!

Let's Remember:

- It *does* matter whose arms hold the child as he grows, because those arms are attached to the person your child is forming a relationship with.

- If you want what's best for your child, provide a stay-at-home parent for at least the first six years of her life.
- Make the most of the time and money you have; learn to budget both responsibly. Your management of these resources will affect your ability to maintain that home court advantage.
- Count the cost of returning to work. One school of thought advises that a parent working outside the home must make two and a half times the price of child care to make that decision economically worthwhile.
- Fathers are biochemically wired to nurture their children at the time of birth, so listen to your body, dads!

12

Give Me a Break

The Home Court Advantage for Single Parents

When balancing work and family in the effort to gain a home court advantage for your children, no one is in a more difficult situation than the single parent. I realize there's not a tougher job in the world. Single parents' lack of time and choice, and the fact that their decisions are often motivated by guilt, can end up turning a difficult situation into something far worse.

But if you love, discipline, and stay close to your child, and make him or her a top priority, you can make it through the difficult times. And you can have homegrown kids.

Those of us who aren't single parents will never really know what it's like to live day after day without any relief in sight from the pressures of single parenting.

What a single mom or dad doesn't have is help and time. You can't invent time; you can't buy it. You can only come up with creative ways to free up more of it, and most single parents will settle for the crumbs of a minute or two scattered here or there.

Some single moms will tell you they'd be thrilled to go potty by themselves in peace and quiet. For many, having part of a day each week that they can call their own happens only in their dreams.

Single mom, I know you feel that life has kicked you in the teeth. I know you didn't expect your husband to die, or ask you for a divorce.

Single dad, I know you didn't want to hear from your friend that he saw your wife with another man.

Neither did your kids wish for any of these scenarios. Now everybody's paying for it.

The question to ask yourself is not "What did I do to deserve this?" It's "What am I going to do with the path ahead?"

As easy as it may be to collapse beside the road, will you keep running the race? You may have been pushed back, but you haven't lost. You and your kids can finish strong, providing you give them the discipline they need; a predictable, safe environment; a healthy dose of Vitamin N (no) and Vitamin E (encouragement); and wise use of the time you *do* have.

Unfortunately, guilt often motivates single parents' child-rearing decisions. They see what other families have and stretch themselves thin trying to keep up. They neglect their own health for the sake of their kids' schedules. They play the "if only" game—*if only* he hadn't cheated on me, *if only* I hadn't gotten pregnant out of wedlock, *if only* I'd gotten that job I interviewed for.

Often the kids make things worse. They point out that they don't have the things others do, making Mom or Dad feel even more guilty.

Because of that guilt, and because single parents can't be home as much, it's easy for them to fall into the activity trap. Or they may have such a demanding schedule that when they get time away from work, they'll do almost anything to get a break. If you're tempted in either of these directions, be vigilant; there are too many harmful influences seducing your child for you to go on autopilot. Value your time together as gold.

Practical Strategies for Low-cost Survival

I've already mentioned the idea of a babysitting co-op. Organizing a group of friends or other parents (single or married) for this purpose is one of the most practical, helpful ways to barter time without cost. Those hours away from your child one morning or afternoon will let you get housework done or relax in the tub or read a book—all without putting your child in preschool.

There are other creative ways to get time off. Connect with other families in your community. Sometimes you have to tell people what your needs are, which isn't always a comfortable thing to do. You might approach a couple you know from church, school, or your son's Cub Scout troop and say, for example, "I know you fish a lot. Is there any way you could take my son fishing with you? I'm not much of a fisherman; I don't know a hook from a line."

If you *aren't* a single parent, you could be the other side of this equation. Look around your church or neighborhood for single moms and dads who need help. Consider offering to take care of a child for an afternoon so that the single parent has a little breathing room.

The Home Court Advantage and Remarriage

If you're a single parent, you may be tempted to convince yourself that you must find someone to marry because you need a spouse and your daughter needs two parents—but don't go there. Many single parents fall in *need* rather than *love*, and end up falling from one lousy relationship to another.

I recommend first raising your kids until they're of age; then, if life is going to include marriage, you're more apt to marry for the right reasons. You probably regret providing a poor example in the first marriage, if it ended in divorce rather than death. But the last thing you want to do is rush into another marriage that may implode.

I'm not laying down an ironclad rule here: "Absolutely do not get remarried until the last kid is out of the house." I simply offer this as a caution.

If you do choose to date, keep your kids away from the man or woman you're seeing until you're certain that the relationship is permanent (not by feelings, but by an actual proposal with a ring and a date). Fight the urge to include your children in a few social situations "to see how they relate."

Listen, your kids aren't guinea pigs to be experimented on. I've seen too many kids bounced around like yo-yos as their single parent dates. Keep in mind that an eighteen-month relationship, followed six months later by a one-year relationship, followed nine months later by a two-year relationship, may seem "stable" to an adult—but to a kid, it feels like having a new parent every time you turn around.

Your Positive Influence

Maybe you sought divorce because your ex-spouse was a negative influence on your kid. You may feel there's no way your child could be "homegrown" given that harmful influence. But hear this: In time, your kids will see the difference between your home and your ex-spouse's home.

You may be tempted to bad-mouth your ex-spouse when your child returns from a weekend at his house; you may be tempted to complain about his latest arrival from the Girlfriend of the Month club; you may be tempted to use your child to spy on him ("What was your dad doing? And was *she* there?"). But if you do, you're asking for trouble in your relationship with your kid.

Don't use your kid to work out your own business. Your spouse may indeed be a bad apple, and your daughter may feel the way you do. But your impressionable 14-year-old's mind will begin defending him, turning him into the dad she wishes she had. She wants him to be different, too, but if you start to tear down her image of what she hopes he could be, she'll start propping it up with fantasies.

Most kids figure out eventually who's involved in their lives, who shows up at their school plays, and who takes the time to listen and talk. Over the years, your son or daughter will most likely see the difference between how you live your life and how your ex-spouse lives his or hers.

Even though you may feel you can't give your child what he needs, he has what's most important if he has your love and affirmation—if he knows you care about him no matter what. That's where your child's self-image starts. Not having both parents in-house may put a child one step behind, but it needn't keep you from succeeding together.

Kids from one-parent homes have become President of the United States, great writers, and founders of large companies. Just as important, many have become productive, nurturing parents who learned to keep their own families together. You *can* beat the odds!

Eight Everyday Ideas

I always urge single parents to take life one day at a time; any more than that can seem too daunting. Many families with two parents and more discretionary time and disposable income fail to set that home court advantage with their children. Your attempt—though possible and worthy—is a difficult one, however you look at it.

That's why I want to close this chapter with some practical strategies. You need extra help to make it.

1. *Hang in there by hanging together.* Children of single parents learn quickly that everybody pitches in—that by age eight or nine when they come home from school, they have to take food out of the freezer in preparation for dinner. That mentality of "It's you and me, kid, against the world" can foster intimacy between single parent and child, and develop emotional fortitude and responsibility.

2. *Be consistent in your discipline.* Since single parents are under extra stress and are tired more often than not, you're likely to respond to circumstances based on your level of exhaustion. Sometimes you'll let a bout of sassing go unheeded, only to "drop the hammer" on the same offense two days later.

I understand how difficult it must be when you never have a relief pitcher, but consistency is a must for children's stability and psychological development. In a calm moment, sit down and decide what your expectations will be; make those expectations known to your children; then enforce them. That may also mean allowing little things (elbows on the table, an occasional belch) to go uncommented on as you focus on what's most important.

3. *Don't let guilt run your life.* The problem with guilt is that it cements you to the past. You can't undo life; focus on the present and the future.

Just because your actions may have put your kids in a less-than-ideal situation, it doesn't mean they should get a toy you can't afford. It doesn't mean they can avoid chores or dress inappropriately. What happened, happened; do your best to deal with the here and now.

4. *Start telling people you love that you need help.* These would be parents, sisters or brothers, and trusted friends. Kids were never meant to be raised alone. While you may not have a husband or wife, look for a grandparent, a sibling, or even a close friend to assist. Beware, though, that you don't overdo allowing others to care for and watch your chil-

dren; otherwise, you reduce your indelible imprint, which is central to having the home court advantage.

5. *Make meals in quantity.* With a group of friends, family members, or neighboring mothers—even by yourself—fix 30 days' worth of meals to freeze for later use. Dinners together are one of the best ways for families to interact, and this tip can make those times more hassle-free.

If you're preparing meals as a group, each person brings a tasty, inexpensive recipe and the necessary ingredients; the group makes a bulk batch of each recipe, which is then divided up to take home. Or have people make the meal in bulk at home, multiplying the quantity for as many people as are gathering; then, when you meet, simply swap meals to take home and freeze. If your children are old enough, do this with them. You might set aside the first Saturday of every month as your "making meals" day, for example.

6. *Take advantage of free activities.* There are plenty of free things single parents can do with their kids. Try story time at the library or bookstore (which may allow you to read on your own or simply have some quiet time), visits to parks, outdoor concerts, etc.

7. *Suggest useful gifts.* When people ask what they can give you for birthdays or Christmas, be practical: "I'd love a certificate for three hours of housecleaning from Merry Maids," or "We'd love a gift certificate to Applebee's." These gifts give you more time together as a family by freeing you from chores.

8. *Let grandparents be grandparents.* Single parents sometimes undermine the "home court" philosophy by letting grandparents become *de facto* parents. You may be so exhausted that when you see the great relief pitcher trotting in from the bullpen—your mom or dad, or both—you feel like saying, "Here, take the ball! Finish this game out."

It's easy to fall into the trap of allowing gracious parents to assume your parental responsibilities; if you're not careful, this transfer can become permanent. Be grateful, but careful in maintaining appropriate boundaries.

Here's an example. Single Mom was going to move in with her parents—just until she got back on her feet. Now she's been there six years, and her oldest child is eleven. At Christmas, Grandma and Grandpa surprise the family with a gift: *We're all going to Disneyland!* The grandparents may think they're doing everyone a favor, but it would have been better to make the reservation for the grandkids and daughter, and let *her* take the kids to Disneyland.

Why? Because Single Mom is becoming her parents' little girl again—in essence, becoming an older sibling to her own children. Perhaps she wants so badly to escape the pressures of parenthood that she surrenders that role. It's easy to become addicted to this kind of "help." But it makes it less likely that your kids will bear your indelible imprint.

Hit a Homegrown Run

If you're a single parent, it's a foregone conclusion that you're not going to be a person of leisure, watching daytime talk shows while you eat bonbons. Yet you can have a homegrown child if you judiciously use the little time you *do* have.

You may be down a couple strikes, but that doesn't mean you can't connect with the next pitch and knock it out of the park. With God's help and your commitment, you *can* pull it off.

Let's Remember:

- Single parenting may be the most difficult job in the world. But instead of asking yourself, "What did I do to deserve this?"

the question to focus on is "What am I going to do with the path laid out ahead of me?"

- Single parents need to create networks of help: parents, friends, and other relatives. Try to find help with basic chores rather than child care, however, so that you can maintain time with your kids and preserve the "home court" philosophy.
- Remarriage is best put off until your kids have left the house. If you feel you must date, do so without involving your kids. It's harmful and inappropriate to ask them to bond with another man or woman who may not be there six months from now.
- Your positive influence can overcome the negative influence of an estranged spouse. Kids may not notice the difference right away, but eventually they will.
- Practical strategies for single parents include being consistent in your discipline, not letting guilt run your life, and telling people you need help.
- Be careful that your parents don't assume the role of parenting your kids. You're still in charge, even if you need help now and then.

PART III

HOME FREE (BUT NOW WHAT?)

13

Making the Transition to a Home Court Advantage

All those childhood days spent fishing in Ellicott Creek taught me that when fish are hooked, they sometimes do something odd—they take to the air. A fish will occasionally break the water's surface and thrash in an attempt to get rid of that fly or lure in its mouth. That fish fights the change, which is exactly what your kids may do when you decide to focus on the home court.

When you radically alter your family's patterns, depending on your children's ages, things are likely to get worse before they get better. I call it the Fish-Out-of-Water Syndrome, because children behave like those creatures, arching their backs psychologically and thrashing in the air.

You can minimize the shock by making the transition carefully. Here are five tips on navigating the passage to a home court advantage.

Tip 1: Don't Expect It to Happen All at Once

I fear that some people may pick up this book and say, "Oh, my, Harold, have we ever missed the boat! That's gotta change *right now.*

"I want everyone in the family room, pronto! Now hear this, now hear this! All leaves are revoked; nobody is going anywhere. We're going to have family night every night of the week, for three hours straight. And we're going to have *fun*. Is that understood?"

If you're running for family president, good luck—because your ratings have just gone down the tube. Good for you that you want to secure that home court advantage for your kids; but it's better to wade into these changes slowly and deliberately, like you're walking into a cold lake. Don't try to reinvent your family's procedures overnight.

For example, let's say your kids are overcommitted to extracurricular activities. As a former dean of students, I always think in semesters; we scheduled our kids for activities a semester at a time. If you're making changes, do that around the kitchen table toward the end of one semester as you begin thinking about the next.

You might start out by saying something like, "Crazy, isn't it? Looking back at the past two months, your dad and I have figured there were exactly four nights that we all sat around this table and had dinner together. We don't want to live that way anymore. In fact, we're not *going* to live that way anymore. We're going to make some changes for you and for us."

If your kids are prepubescent, that may be just fine with them. If they're older, however, that may cause some struggle. If you decide to make changes to balance work and family, then announce to your 15-year-old son that you're suddenly available and expect him to be home more often as well, don't kid yourself—he isn't going to do backflips in celebration. That boy will have to radically adjust as he learns to relate to you and deal with his feelings about your emotional absence and the reality of a more intimate relationship. Bit by bit, however, you can begin to re-enter his world.

If you pare down from four activities to one per semester, and your kids are hooked on the pattern, there's likely to be an outcry: "It's not fair!"

"You know what?" you could tell them. "You're right. It's not fair for Dad and me to be in a total of eight activities per month. Your father works all day at the office and I work all day at home. So we're not going to play this game any longer. You'll have to make some choices about what you're going to do next semester. You don't have to decide tonight, but we need to know in the next few weeks so we can make plans."

They may howl like stuck pigs.

"Kids," you can say, "when you're older and you want to get involved in more activities, go for it. But for now, this is too stressful for our family. We're going to save money and effort; we're going to chill out more."

Who knows? You might even start talking to each other.

As these changes take place, you need to be the adult with a capital "A." That is, you need to be objective and wise and recognize that what your kids may perceive as a threat is really a gift.

Tip 2: Make Sure It's "All for One and One for All"

I love it when farmers attend my seminars.

"You can go home," I tell them. "There's nothing new I can teach you about maintaining the home court advantage. Nearly everything you need to know, you learned on the farm."

In a family that takes advantage of the home court, everybody works and everybody pitches in—just as it is on the farm. This should be true whether you live in downtown Manhattan or among the wheat fields of the Midwest. Pitching in creates one of the most important gifts you can give your children: a sense of belonging. Without that, you'll find making the switch to "homegrowing" difficult indeed.

In our culture, unfortunately, too many families live as if parents exist solely for the independent advancement of each child. When the family acts as if a daughter's or son's worth depends on what he or she can do *outside* the home, the children have a correspondingly weaker sense of belonging *inside* the home.

If you treat your eight-year-old like a future Olympian or Metropolitan Opera singer in training—doing all his chores, cleaning his room, taking care of his laundry so he can focus on his "special talent"—you may think you're giving him every advantage. But you're depriving him of the most important advantage: the sense of being a vital part of the family unit. You may end up turning that shining star into a falling star by the time he leaves home.

For a family to truly take advantage of the home court, everybody must sacrifice; the family adds up to more than the sum of its parts. And all members of a family are important: The straight-A student is no more valuable or loved than the C-student class clown. The gifted athlete isn't more important than the shy, chubby lastborn.

A child growing up in a home like that knows she may be cut from the team, fired from her job, or kicked out of a club—but she'll always belong to the family. There will always be a place for her at the table, a bed for her to sleep on. More importantly, there will always be a group of people who'll support her, love her, and encourage her.

As a 60-year-old father of a 12-year-old, I don't take this for granted. It gives me great pleasure to know that when I'm in an old folks' home, drooling on my walker and putting my underwear on backwards and inside out, Holly, Krissy, and Kevin will be looking after their two younger sisters. Marriage may change the girls' last names—but they'll always be Lemans, and the Lemans will always stick together.

Always.

How do you build this sense of togetherness and belonging? By living life together; that's what defines family! That's the whole idea! If Sammy is at baseball while Susie is at ballet while Sharon is at soccer while Stevie is at Cub Scouts, you're just creating a common place to hang your clothes until you leave home the next morning.

Should you reward your kids for pitching in by paying them in addition to their allowance? No. Dad doesn't get paid for helping when the dishes need washing, nor does Mom get a bonus for balancing the checkbook. Neither should your kids.

Fortunately, taking responsibility can have its own rewards. If your 12-year-old daughter comes home from school and remembers her job to pull dinner out of the freezer, she won't have to answer to a ravenous pack of family members that evening.

The Three Amigos, like the Three Musketeers, had it right: All for one and one for all! That's how "home court" children are trained in selflessness.

Tip 3: Don't Fall Back into the Trap

Once you've decided to get out of the activity trap, it takes work to *stay* out and to handle the adjustments the transition brings. If you've begun putting the principles of this book into practice, you may be finding that getting the family to embrace a simpler life together is as easy as herding cats.

Take heart; the transition is never easy. Busyness is as addictive as caffeine and sugar. Teenagers in particular, who are often quite comfortable with the frenetic pace, may have a difficult time cutting back. You may find it challenging yourself to avoid slipping back into the trap as you fear your kids aren't reaching their potential. The truth is that putting them back in endless activities would *keep* them from reaching their potential.

I know, I know—that sounds backwards. Other parents may accuse you of robbing your children when you begin to pull them out of the trap: "What do you mean Sarah is dropping out of the traveling basketball squad? I tell you, that girl is a player! But she'll never get a college scholarship if she just bumps shoulders with those citywide rec players. She needs the competition!"

If your child is involved in too many activities, she won't reach her potential in anything. She'll lack the core value of belonging to something (the family) based on who she *is* (a beloved daughter and sister), not on what she *does* (score points, play an instrument, get top grades).

Besides, does having more options really help your child narrow down what's most important to her? By limiting your child's activities to one per term, your child has to choose. Giving kids that focus encourages them to home in on their passions more effectively than trying out everything the planet has to offer.

If you're banking on higher college placement by encouraging all those activities, think again. To college admissions personnel, extracurricular activities aren't all we make them out to be. "In a survey on recruiting trends conducted [in 2000] by the National Association for College Admission Counseling, 'work and extracurricular activities' ranked 11th in a list of factors influencing admissions decisions—far below grades, test scores, and class rank."[1]

Those who laud other benefits of extracurricular activities might cite teamwork or responsibility. Those are good reasons, I suppose, but guess what? All those traits can be developed within the family as well.

If you find yourself sliding back into the activity trap, ask yourself why. Is it because you have a "shining star" at home? Does that member of the family dominate the family's schedule? This is easy to slip into if you have a particularly gifted kid. But it's not fair to the others when a family devotes so much time and energy to one member.

The problem with a "bright light" is that it can wipe out all the little lights. If you want a homegrown family, don't allow one child's gifts to eclipse the development of all the other children.

On the other hand, you may be sneaking back into the trap because you like the accolades. Take Marge, for instance:

"Marge," notes a neighbor, "you homeschool all four of your kids, *and* you take them to swimming, ballet, piano, and soccer!"

"Oh, it's nothing," Marge replies. "They're my priority, after all!"

"But you've been out all day shuttling the kids from one end of town to the other."

"Well, we do put more than our share of miles on the minivan, and the kids certainly do keep me busy. But I manage."

"Marge," the neighbor says, filled with admiration, "how *do* you do it?"

As one who subtly relishes her role as martyr, Marge clearly requires a regular ego massage. But the Super Mom act isn't helping her family a bit.

Let's be honest—there's an emotional payoff for a parent when others take notice. But when we're sacrificing our kids' futures to have our egos stroked, the cost is too high!

When that next opportunity comes knocking—and it will—there's only one way to keep from stepping back into the activity trap.

Learn to say *no.*

It's not difficult; go ahead, say it: "No."

Sorry—that was a little soft. Be firmer this time: "*No!*"

There you go. That one spoken word has the remarkable ability to shut the door on whatever you're asked to participate in, lead, or give to.

Having that home court advantage for your children isn't a one-time decision; it's committing to a day-by-day pattern of countercultural choices that focus on the priorities of family and simple living.

There will always be people trying to lasso you into their projects. While one here or there is worth considering, the truth is that we can't do them all.

Saying *no* takes practice. When asked, many don't have the foresight to say, "I'll think about it. Let me ask my mate," or, "Let me check my schedule. I'll get back to you." That delay buys you time, provides objective distance between you and the person asking, and lets you and your spouse decide together what you can live with a few months down the road.

When you come back with your *no*, start your sentence with that word. "No. It sounds like a great program, and I wish I could help, but I have other commitments." The shorter you can make that response, the better. Be gentle but firm, confident that you're making wise decisions for your family. Otherwise, that well-intentioned person looking for volunteers may read your hesitancy as indecision, and try again to pull you in.

Saying no can be incredibly healthy for your family. That's why I call it Vitamin N.

Tip 4: Make the Hard Choices

Sometimes your kids need Vitamin N, too. It can be tough to give it to them, especially if the idea is new to you. But if you want to shift focus to the home court, you have to make countercultural decisions that some parents blindly allow others to make for them.

Let's say your son or daughter is going to the seventh grade formal. Other parents think it's a great idea to rent a stretch limo. I think it's an appalling idea, and I don't mind telling anyone who asks. Don't get caught up in going along with other families in a case like that.

Consider another example. Are you going to say, "Oh, I guess it's okay for my fifth grade son to see that movie. Everyone's seeing it"? An all-you-can-eat buffet of movies isn't the healthiest thing for kids. Some films are violent; others glorify values you probably want to discourage. I'm not going to pay someone $8 so that he can have an hour and 45 minutes to drill into my children's heads what I'm trying to rid them of.

The earlier you develop a pattern of setting and maintaining healthy boundaries with Vitamin N, the better off you'll be when the kids enter adolescence and begin taking more responsibility for themselves. Remember, you're the parent; he's the child.

This reminds me of the parent who occasionally approaches me during a weekend seminar, complaining about her kid who eats too much junk food.

"What junk food does he eat, ma'am?" I'll reply.

"Ice cream. He's always in the ice cream; he inhales the stuff."

"Where does he get the ice cream?"

"I buy it at the grocery store."

"So you're telling me that *you* are the one buying all the ice cream that you don't want your child to eat?"

"Uh . . . yeah."

Parent, you have to draw those lines. Don't let something as frivolous as junk food or entertainment undercut the benefits of homegrown living. In the case of movies, if there's one that's even close to being a risk, Sande or I will see it with our daughters or they're not going to see it at all. We're responsible for them, and that means being there to correct a message that contradicts our family's values. (Incidentally, one of Focus on the Family's Web sites, www.pluggedinonline.com, offers resources for evaluating movies' language, sexual content, and violence.)

"You're a Leman," I tell my kids, "and we're not like everybody else." There are certain things I'm not going to let them do, and they know it; they'd never say, "But Daddy, everybody's doing it."

Saying *no* when necessary helps homegrown kids to be healthy kids, even if they aren't always happy about it.

That doesn't mean you *always* say no, of course. Case in point: If an older kid—say, age 14—objects to going somewhere with the rest of the family, you might let her stay home. "We're going to miss you," you might say, then go on your way. Not everybody likes the same activities; at times, using common sense, you give your child space.

Sometimes, though, you have to make an executive decision for the family. Move gently but swiftly, even firmly. Hear out objections, because love doesn't demand its own way. But then make the call.

For instance, you may tell your 14-year-old that the family is going to Aunt Matilda's house for Thanksgiving. He may respond, "But I hate going to Aunt Matilda's house!"

"Honey, you can hate it all you want," you reply. "I understand. But we've been invited as a family and we're going as a family."

"But, Dad, I'm going to be miserable all day."

"I know you'll be miserable. I understand what that's like. But going to Aunt Matilda's will be good for you; it'll make you appreciate the next day when you're not there."

At times you might attempt redirection, putting a positive spin on the outing. My doctor does that, trying to take my mind off the fact that I hate colonoscopies by making NASCAR noises as he's using the probe.

"Okay, we're in the straightaway . . . and now a hard left turn," he'll say, then make the sound of squealing tires. That lightens the process, though the fact remains that I'm not keen on colonoscopies.

If it's clear that a visit with Aunt Matilda really is a miserable prospect to your child, just acknowledge that there are some things in life we simply don't enjoy. Neither his "misery" nor your empathy changes the fact that your child doesn't have to enjoy the outing to join the family. Perhaps you say to your son, "We don't ask you to do many things, but this is one trip you need to join. I know it's not fun, but it's a nonnegotiable."

Giving your kids everything they want may produce fleeting happiness. But encouraging a greater commitment to your family's values by sometimes saying *no* produces healthy, homegrown children.

Tip 5: Keep Adjusting the Boundaries

When kids are learning to walk, you hold their hands to let them practice placing one foot in front of the other. In time, they learn the balance required to walk on their own. Then you hold their hands again to teach them safety when crossing streets. Eventually they learn to look both ways and navigate traffic themselves.

In other words, you hold them close—then let them go.

That season-by-season, back-and-forth process of your comforting presence—alternating with your confident encouragement to step into the world—marks the growth of healthy children. Your role changes not just during your transition to focus on the home court, but again and again through the years as your child prepares to one day hit the road.

When your kid is young and inexperienced, you don't just let him go and do his own thing. As he gets older and begins discovering his own identity, you open your hands to let him take those first tentative steps in a direction. He'll fall down at times, and you hold him again.

You can't keep him from those bumps and bruises of trying; he must learn through his failures as well as his successes. When kids ultimately leave home, you want them to be self-sufficient, to have gathered the skills needed to make it on their own, and to love others with the same love they received at home.

But how do you know if you're holding your kids *too* closely? Many adults who grew up in dysfunctional families don't know what a healthy parental presence is. They overcompensate in their attempts to break the pattern. That's why you see "hover" parents who smother their kids. But neither hovering nor showering kids with opportunities and material things will create children who learn self-sufficiency and an outward focus. Those approaches create kids who are babied, who only care about their own backsides.

"Holding them close" comes easily to most moms and dads. "Letting go" is more difficult, especially for first-time parents. It's natural to hold that first, precious life a bit more closely than the child needs to be held; parenting is so new and your baby seems so fragile. But as you find that ingested dirt isn't lethal and that your child has the resiliency of a rubber ball, you can begin to loosen up.

If you're wondering whether you're holding your child too closely, ask yourself the following questions:

1. Whose needs are being met in the way I relate to my child? If *my* needs are the motivating factor, what will I do to change that?

2. Is the money I spend on my child's activities a form of smothering her with the things I never had?

3. Are my choices regarding my child's life leading us to a simpler, more balanced, disciplined, family-centered lifestyle?

The Rocky, Rewarding Road

Homegrown children are worth it. The transition away from the activity trap isn't always easy, and can be rocky. The earlier you establish simple, family-centered routines, the easier it will be.

Regardless of whether your children are 15 months old or 15 years old, though, be sure you make that transition. There's no time like the present for committing to maintain that home court advantage.

Let's Remember:

- When you radically change your family's patterns, depending on your children's ages, things are likely to get worse before they get better. Make changes in your family's routine slowly.
- All members of a family are important. But a family adds up to more than the sum of its parts.
- "Home court" kids have responsibilities at home; by pitching in, they begin to take ownership of the family and feel a crucial sense of belonging.
- Don't fall back into the activity trap by letting one member of the family dominate the family's time, which is easy to do if you have a particularly gifted kid.
- Avoid falling back into the activity trap for the sake of your parental ego, which perpetuates the myth that "I'm a good parent because I make tremendous sacrifices for my children."
- Raising "home court" kids isn't a one-time decision; it's committing to a day-by-day pattern of countercultural choices to focus on the priority of simple living.
- "Home court" kids may not always be happy kids. But they'll be healthier as you refuse them what they're better off without and generously provide what they need.
- The back-and-forth process of your comforting presence alternating with your confident encouragement marks the growth of healthy children. Hold them close, then let them go.

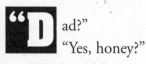

Up With Downtime

Creativity and the Value of Boredom

"**D**ad?"

"Yes, honey?"

"I'm bored."

"You are?"

"Yeah."

"Really, *really* bored?"

"Yeah. I'm really, really, *really* bored."

"Wow. It'll be fun seeing what you decide to do to get out of that."

My daughter looked at me like I'd just grown three noses and two more ears. She was at a loss for words, so I explained what was going on.

"I'm not your activity director, honey. You have lots of games, you can play with the dog, you can talk to your sister—and I can't wait to see what you decide to do. It'll be fun for me to watch."

Escaping the activity trap creates "downtime." To the busy parent downtime may seem like the Holy Grail, but to your children it may feel like torture. Be very, very careful how you handle what happens next.

One of the chief temptations upon escaping the activity trap can be to replace activity *outside* the home with activity *inside* the home. Once you've stepped back and created space in your family's schedule, the question you must face is this: Will you keep time open for spontaneous family interaction, or will you rush to fill the vacuum?

There are some helpful, practical things you can do with your new-found time at home, which we'll discuss in Chapter 14. But first, let's talk about one of the best things you can do with those hours if you want that home court advantage for your children: *nothing!*

Give Them Room to Breathe!

Life isn't meant to be lived pillar to post. If you want "home court" children, you must allow for downtime so that your family isn't stressed at every turn.

"A study by the University of Michigan quantified the downtime deficit; in the last 20 years American kids have lost about four unstructured hours a week."[1] Opening your family's schedule—and *leaving* some of it open—gives your child time he needs to form his self-awareness and identity.

Downtime is not "free" time. When those calls come asking you to volunteer, not having anything scheduled doesn't mean you should feel guilty for turning them down. Your family needs unscheduled time; protect it as much as you would any other event.

That's true even if you don't have anything planned—other than your plan to leave room for what comes up with your family. Needs will always arise at home: help with homework, trips to the store for school supplies, conversations on why watching a certain television show isn't healthy.

Time to Call Time Out?

Kids need downtime—we all do. It's not just for toddlers desperate for an afternoon rest despite their protests to the contrary. "I know it's time for downtime when Max starts to suck his thumb," said one mother of her 11-month-old. "It doesn't necessarily mean he's sleepy; he may simply want to go in his crib and veg out."[2]

How can you tell if your child needs more downtime? Look for signs of exhaustion. If you go for a ride in the car, is she asleep before you've driven a half mile? Is his face planting in his mashed potatoes at dinner?

Fatigue is a natural part of growing up, of course. And kids will tire more easily as their bodies develop and they adjust to transitions at school and elsewhere. But is your child's schoolwork sliding when he used to stay on top of it pretty well? Does she seem listless, or talk less than she did before? Is he saying things like, "I just want to quit!"? If you hear or see signs like these, take time to evaluate whether your child may be overwhelmed.

Take a look at your child's schedule. Is it nonstop? It shouldn't be. Some people advocate the year-round school, for example, but I'm a traditionalist who believes kids need summers off. When I was growing up, every summer my friends and I built a raft in the creek near my house; every summer, without fail, our raft sank. None of us ended up as an engineer, but it was important for us to try. We invented games, held our own contests, and organized events in the neighborhood. The initiative we learned through those activities was invaluable.

Today's kids have their lives so scheduled and mapped out for them, with scarcely an afternoon or evening off, that many have lost the ability to get out and build a raft or create a "pie" out of pine needles, dandelions, and mud. That's sad; the way back is to insist on a schedule where these activities become possible.

When you schedule downtime, your kids may whine and complain and lie around for a few days. But eventually—if you monitor the video games, computer time, and television—they'll rediscover the glory of being kids with an empty day in front of them. I don't think kids have changed; it's parents and their poor priorities that have gotten us where we are.

You're Better Than a Video

"But won't downtime lead to vegetating?" you might ask. "Don't kids need the stimulation they get from activities and games and CDs and TV?" You might be surprised at the answer.

One mom fondly remembers the many times she awakened with her 18-month-old son sitting on top of her, using her body as a highway for his Hot Wheels cars. He had an entire house to play in, but the one road he thought would be *really* fun to drive was the one leading, quite literally, to his mother's heart!

Many parents buy all sorts of games for their kids in an attempt to stimulate their development. But if you watch your baby closely, her eyes ultimately follow you as you move from one place in the kitchen to the next. Your child knows your voice; she's tuned in to *you*. "Try to remember that bonding results from a baby's feeling secure about his parents' love and response to his needs, not from doing things together," says Lise Eliot, Ph.D.[3] *You* are the one who stimulates your child the most.

The best thing for your child, more than educational toys or videos, is a relaxed atmosphere in which you talk and sing to him, hold him, and read those cloth books (the ones that double as hors d'oeuvres for babies) as you point at the pictures of the colored balloons and the man and the cow.

This is one area where I honestly believe parents with less money have an advantage. Because they can't afford computer programs, expensive games and mobiles, or cable television, they may feel their children are deprived. But any baby will take a walking, breathing, active mommy or daddy (or even better, both) over any toy ever invented.

The *worst* trade you could make would be to remove both parents from the home and send them to work so that Junior or Missy could have a few more toys. The best stimulation is, and always will be, *you*.

"Mom, There's Nothing to Do!"

Does being your child's primary stimulus mean you're supposed to serve as a 24/7 activity coordinator? No. You aren't the *only* stimulation. Sometimes you even need to let kids grow through boredom.

I remember growing that way when I was five years old. I sprawled on my bed, "doing nuthin'." I suppose I could have been outside playing, helping Mom in the kitchen, or doing a whole host of other things. But I was bored in that midsummer's way, as only a child caught between the thrill of school's end and the anticipation of school's beginning can be.

As I lay there, I heard a faint buzzing—barely audible—far away. I lay motionless as the buzz grew in volume, slowly, like a mosquito gathering up courage. As it grew louder I recognized it as a small, single-engine airplane flying across the sky. Somehow that sound captivated my imagination so much that those minutes hang in my memory like a cherished photo.

In my book *Unlocking the Secrets of Your Childhood Memories*, I've written about how some of our earliest memories provide clues to who we are: our loves, our dislikes, our personalities. Back then I must have had inklings of how nice it would be to travel. The buzz of that airplane's engine must have triggered something in me that carried me beyond the four walls of my bedroom.

When I was a kid, my family didn't travel much. We took two vacations; one lasted a week and one lasted a weekend—and both were visits to the same lake in western New York where my family still vacations to this day. The sound of that engine must have awakened something that was part of me all along: a sense of adventure, the desire to see new places and meet new people.

Boredom isn't intrinsically bad. It's not a monster to fend off with an arsenal of CDs, DVDs, and Xbox video games. Give your schedule a little room to breathe and boredom will move in like a fog—with potentially helpful results.

I remember one conversation with Lauren, who was six years old at the time.

"I'm bored," she said with a slouch that suggested she was carrying the weight of the world.

"That's okay, honey," I replied. "You can be bored. You can be bored all day. When you're done being bored, welcome back to life."

Boredom puts kids in touch with reality; it lets them know that the world usually isn't a three-ring circus. To this day, Lauren is probably the most independent of our kids, content to amuse herself.

A parent's job is not to entertain the children. There's no satisfying a child's appetite for the latest, most amusing activities anyway. Yet because many moms and dads today are uncomfortable with "dead air," they feel the need to fill that void with something—*anything*.

But crucial development happens in that void for both child and adult. That silence allows us to get in touch with what's going on inside ourselves: our search for meaning, identity, and answers to unresolved questions; our frustrations; our pains; and our future direction. By taking the time to sit in silence, pondering questions and facing doubts and fears, we grow emotionally and spiritually.

That downtime allows kids time to sort things out, to process life around them. They can contemplate a sunbeam coming through a window and the dust that dances on the air, wonder about the natural world, and consider deeper questions like, "What am I good at?" "What will I be when I grow up?" or "Will I ever get married?"

The dream I had as a five-year-old, to travel, came true. Now I frequently find myself on planes or driving along freeways in rented cars as I head to or from conferences to speak. I don't dread that time alone; on the contrary, I love it because it gives me a chance to think. At home, I relish days when I can just bum around, puttering away at the little items on my list because of the empty day stretching before me. Relaxed days are a rare treat, and I cherish them as gifts. So do "home court" families.

Making Something from Nothing

"In our efforts to produce Renaissance children who are competitive in all areas," said Dr. Diane Ehrensaft, developmental and clinical psychologist and professor at The Wright Institute in Berkeley, "we squelch creativity."[4] Ironic, isn't it, that the very parents who push their children to succeed may be failing in one of the areas that matters most—creativity?

To grow in creativity, your family needs downtime. You must practice the fine (and often boring) art of sitting with nothing. Creativity, after all, is the art of making something from thin air. Whether it's an empty page or a blank canvas, nothing—that favorite haunt of boredom—is the beginning of any creative endeavor.

Kids need time to reach that stretching point of boredom, then to wrestle with creativity. Watching a movie or playing Nintendo may touch the imagination, but that's not the same as *creating* something from the imagination. Someday your child will be drafting a business plan from scratch, planning new curriculum for the classroom, or working on a television show, as my son, Kevin II, is. Letting kids press through their boredom into something they can get excited about is good training.

What will your child do with his free time? Preschoolers may choose a pile of blankets and chairs to build tunnels; pubescent kids may make lemonade stands, organize neighborhood carnivals, publish a newspaper, or stage plays for parents and friends. Give your child a pile of scrap wood to build a fort in the backyard, the ingredients to make chocolate chip cookies, or, if she's old enough, a video camera to go outside and make her own movie.

Creativity can be a messy prospect; I heard of one young boy who was heard yelling instructions across the yard to his friend who held a garden hose. "No, not like that!" the boy shouted. "You have to get wet first and *then* roll in the dirt!" Only a kid would come up with the best recipe for getting mud to stick to clothes.

When I grew up, that kind of play with buddies was an essential part of life. We didn't have great equipment—we wrapped baseballs in electrical tape, for Pete's sake. We produced plays, formed a circus, and ran track and field games. We even organized a league for kids on our street to play baseball against kids on a neighboring street; it lasted only two games over the course of a week, but the point was that *we* created something.

Children don't always need regimented activities. They need unstructured time, downtime—with the TV off, joining Dad and Mom to read a book or work on a project together.

Kids need time to be creative. As Leonardo Da Vinci said, "Men of genius do most when they work least."

You tell 'em, Leo!

Independence: Going It Alone

At age 10, I had my own commercial garden where I grew fruits and veggies, then sold them at a street stand to make a few extra cents. Red raspberries were 60 cents per quart; my homegrown tomatoes were a mere 50 cents per quart!

I must confess that my produce wasn't *all* the result of my own hard work. On the grounds of a local institution, I did find some currant bushes that no one picked. Every year the currants withered and were eaten by birds, so I made the logical business move of a 10-year-old and added them to my inventory. Needless to say, I had pretty low overhead in the currant market.

That time I spent "building my business" helped me develop self-sufficiency and business skills that I benefit from today. When one of my books is released, I get more enjoyment from thinking about how to market it than I do from any other aspect of the process. The best-written book in the world won't mean much if nobody reads it; and how will anybody think to read it if somebody doesn't tell them about it?

My parents gave me a fair amount of leeway, perhaps more than many who live in the city or suburbs would give their kids today. My mother likes to tell the story of how she would wake up and find the note I'd written for her before I left for the woods, sometimes even before sunrise. "Don't worry," I'd write, "I've gone to the creek and I'll be back before school." I always added, "P.S. I'm dressed warmly."

Living in a rural town without the dazzle of city life probably helped me grow in independence. That isn't to say that if you reside in

Chicago you should pack up and move to Leech, Arkansas. But the bigger your city, the more opportunities for organized activities—which you may have to resist in order to give your child the downtime that develops self-sufficiency.

I know that today, in many of the places we live, that kind of broad freedom is neither possible nor safe. But by trusting your child with time to explore, play, and create within the boundaries of his world, you communicate, "I believe in you; I know you can handle this situation."

You Have Your Rest Cut Out for You

"Out of gas?" your church bulletin reads. "Come here to refuel!"

Refuel? you may be thinking. *How about helping me off the racetrack?*

Unfortunately, in many communities of faith, overwork isn't discouraged—it's applauded. Sundays, traditionally a time for families to rest, drive in the country, and enjoy nature's beauty together, have become a harried pit stop on life's Indy 500. For many families, Sunday is now the day to catch up on laundry, clean the bathroom, or wash the car.

Having a day set aside for rest is a good thing, if only we follow through with it. Each week, try to take a day off completely from work at home or at the job.

By taking that stand, you'll be embracing what people have recognized throughout the ages: We all need downtime!

Let's Remember:

- You're the best stimulation for your child—though that doesn't mean being his or her 24/7 activity coordinator.

- One of the chief temptations upon escaping the activity trap can be to replace activity *outside* the home with activity *inside* the home. Opening time for your family and leaving some of it open gives your child the opportunity to form his self-awareness and identity.
- To grow in creativity, kids must practice the fine (and often boring) art of sitting around with nothing to do. Creativity, after all, is the art of making something from nothing; downtime is the necessary environment for that to happen.
- We all need downtime. It allows the body to rest and the mind to process all it's taken in. It develops independence. It helps us grow emotionally and spiritually. Try to take a day off completely once per week from work at home or elsewhere.

The "Home Court" Marriage

Foundation of a Family with

a Home Court Advantage

Nicolas Copernicus' idea was simple, but revolutionary: The Sun, not the Earth, lies at the center of our solar system.

Today, no thinking person would dispute this. But at the time, Copernicus' idea rocked the world scientifically and theologically. People had assumed that everything revolved around the Earth, a view that seemed to fit the scientific data as well as religious beliefs of the day. Humans were, of course, at the center of it all.

Many parents today live under a similar illusion. They think that believing in your child means making him the center of your family.

That may seem at first the noble and loving thing to do. But making your child the family's center—perhaps putting your relationship with your spouse on hold for 18 years—spells trouble.

A *family-centered child* rather than a *child-centered family* produces a more giving person. If you're a family with a faith and everything centers around giving your child Disneyland on Earth, will he or she understand the need for God? That child is likely to develop sky-high expectations—namely, that his well-being is primary and all else is secondary. If your aim is to raise a child who'll look out for others before himself, you've missed the mark.

You want to communicate that you're there for your child. You don't want to go too far and communicate that you're there *only* for your child.

Thankfully, God has created another institution within the family that naturally balances this out.

It's called marriage.

"How Come We Can't Come?"

I hate bed and breakfasts.

They just aren't me. After I've sat still as a choirboy on three flights and endured two layovers watching the same looping airport CNN newscast, when I finally arrive in my room, all I really want is a comfortable place to rest. In a bed and breakfast, I'm afraid to sit on any of the furniture because I don't want to break great-grandmother's antique rocking chair. I can live without sleeping on a pile of goose feathers. And even though I love people, I'm not keen on having lively, early morning discussion with other couples from Des Moines and Anchorage.

But my antique-loving wife really likes the bed and breakfasts. So on a recent anniversary we took off for a nice one—so nice that even I ended up liking it. Before we left home, however, Hannah and Lauren bombarded us with questions.

"How come we can't come?" they asked.

I thought, *I'm about to do things with your mother that would make you blush several times over*. But my reply was, "There are times when Mom and Dad need to be alone."

"Why?" asked Lauren.

"Honey," I told her, "I know it may be hard for you to understand, but we had a relationship before we had any of you. And this is our way of keeping that relationship close. You know how sometimes you like to go out to your favorite restaurant with just me?"

"Yeah."

"Well, your mother is the same way."

It's hard for a young kid to imagine that her parents had a relationship before she came on the scene. Lauren's history of the world began just before the Clinton administration. But because I don't want my personal life to resemble that administration, I'm determined to spend time nurturing my marriage!

Getting away isn't just for me and Sande. It's for Hannah and Lauren, too—as well as my older kids, especially Krissy, who's married and has a child of her own. She continues to watch what her parents do to make their marriage matter.

These encounters tell my children that marriage is important, and that husbands and wives need to get away. My actions communicate that, as much as I love my kids, the apple of my eye always has been and always will be my lovely bride. Sande is the woman who caught my eye before the dawn of time (in my kids' view), and she'll be the one walking by my side when they're raising families of their own.

This doesn't mean, of course, that going off for a romantic getaway is always easy. If you've ever left a child behind for the weekend, you probably can relate to the following experience.

The first night it's as if you're running through a field of wildflowers in soft-focus lighting. You can't believe it. You eat in a restaurant where the suffix "meal" isn't tacked on to the end of each entrée, and dinner conversation breaks the sound barrier into three-syllable words. Waiting for your food is actually part of the experience, not a breeding ground for a minivan riot. Later that evening you have a wonderful sexual interlude without fear of Munchkin representatives from the Lollipop Guild knocking on your door or overhearing a few gasps or sighs.

The second day, your rejuvenated minds begin making the turns down that carpool route.

"So, it's 11:30 A.M. Grandma ought to be picking Little Peanut up from preschool."

"Yeah, I wonder what he did today."

"Well, it's the beginning of Letter 'T' Week. Mrs. Johnson was supposed to bring Jamie's pet tarantula this morning."

"The letter 'T,' huh?" you ruminate. "That was always one of my favorite letters."

By the third day, you can't wait to get away from your getaway to get your hands on your kids.

But it's good to have time alone together, even if it's just putting your kids to bed early so that the two of you can catch up. Mike Mason, in his book *The Mystery of Marriage*, describes the demands of a marital relationship as a "big, powerful, shiny, eight-cylinder gas guzzler that has to be kept constantly on the road."[1] Marriage does take an incredible amount of time and energy. Nevertheless, it's worth giving the attention it requires. Otherwise, you'll find the two of you, along with the rest of the family, stuck along the highway of life in a broken-down relationship.

This doesn't have to be expensive. Take a walk in a new neighborhood, talking about houses you like and don't like, and dream about what your own might look like someday. Dust off that Scrabble box or rent a classic movie. It's about changing the pace and priorities of your life.

Couple Power

One of the best ways to nurture your children is to nurture your relationship with your spouse. It produces what I call "Couple Power," and it's a stabilizing factor in your child's life. If you don't develop and protect this pattern early on, your child will suffer—and 18 years down the road you'll be looking across a restaurant table trying to remember your spouse's middle name.

I recommend starting some habits at the beginning of your child's life. Within the first few weeks, when he or she is still getting used to navigating a world outside amniotic fluid, leave that child alone with a trusted relative or friend for a couple hours so that the two of you can have an evening alone.

Dr. Leman, you might be thinking, *how can you be so calloused when that helpless newborn needs his parents?*

Hear me out. This excursion does three things:

1. It sends a gentle message to Little Peanut—namely, that Dad and Mom's time together is important. It says, "As much as we love you, you are not the center of the universe; everything does not revolve around you."

2. It sets a pattern of developing and maintaining Couple Power, that growing intimacy in your relationship.

3. It enables Little Peanut to sense the love between you and your spouse. When the two of you stand strong together, your child gains confidence that his home is a stable place.

The first time you leave your child behind, she'll probably freak out. The voices around her change, the chest she's up against feels different, and service may be a bit slow when she places her order for milk.

But in a couple hours she'll find her concern was a false alarm—when you return to the family, stronger than ever, to love her.

Intimacy: That Priceless Jewel

Take one picture-perfect marriage. Add a second job on top of the first to maintain your choice lifestyle; fold in the hope of a promotion.

For her, season liberally with commitments to lead the church women's ministry and sing in a choir or two; for him, stir in coaching a soccer team that travels frequently, plus regular weekends fishing with his buddies. Add a kid or two, with three or four extracurricular activities each. Shake well.

For any family, this is a dangerous recipe for alienation. For the "home court" family, it's of special concern because it can eventually lead to the breakup of family bonds.

Ask the parents in this scenario about their relationship. Ask whether they have time to go on a date. If they're honest, you're likely to get the familiar answer, "No—but if we did, I'm afraid we wouldn't have anything to talk about."

Intimacy is a priceless jewel. It can't be purchased for any amount, and can only be given freely. To put it another way, it's like a rose. You can no more force a relationship than you can force a rosebud to bloom. Intimacy takes time; there's no quick way to grow it. And when we begin putting activities or the pursuit of lavish lifestyles above relationships, the entire family suffers.

That's because intimacy is the foundation of your family. If your marriage goes, everything will be blown to bits—the stability your children depend upon, the sense of belonging they thrive on, and the sense of security they feed on.

Marital intimacy isn't built merely on grand gestures, however, such as an occasional weekend away. You also need to sprinkle in constant affirmation. Silence isn't golden to intimacy's ears. Many spouses will seek words and gestures of affection from others when they can't get them at home.

If you're too busy running the kids around and juggling responsibilities, you may not be cruel to your spouse. But you're probably neglectful. Some evening you'll go to bed and think to yourself, *When was the last time we even made love?*

Let me tell you the Leman rule for this: If you can't remember the last time, *it's been way too long!*

The ability to raise children with a home court advantage depends on your ability to support and affirm your spouse. It's from that strength of intimacy that you love your children more fully.

Live the Life

At root, the "home court" philosophy is this: Live the life you want your child to live.

Do you want her to slowly grow distant from her spouse until the two of them have nothing in common anymore, and one of them finally has an affair? Or do you want their relationship to grow ever deeper and more meaningful as the years pass?

When I take Sande away from our children for a weekend, I'm giving the girls a lifetime lesson: Husbands should cherish and romance their wives. And guess what? When some loser guy tries to treat them like dirt, their first thought will be, *Hey, that's not the way men are supposed to treat women! I remember how Dad took care of Mom. That's what I want. Get out of here!*

Take time for each other. If you have to, *make* time. That means giving something up. Keep each other first in your heart and affection.

It's a terrible lesson to act as if your spouse's needs come last. If you do that, your child may treat his or her mate the same way—and that mate may not be so gracious or patient as yours. A satisfied spouse makes a much more involved and loving parent than a neglected one does.

My goal for our kids is this: I hope, on the day I die, that each kid will say, "Secretly, I always thought Daddy loved me the best, but I also always knew he loved Mommy the most."

That, in my dictionary, is the definition of a family with a true home court advantage.

Let's Remember:

- Having a *family-centered child* rather than a *child-centered family* produces a more giving person.
- As a couple, don't be afraid to take time away from your kids. Whether it's a romantic weekend getaway or just putting them to bed early so you can talk, they need the example as well as the energy you'll gain from recharging your relationship.
- The ability to raise "home court" children depends on your ability to support and affirm your spouse. It's from that strength of intimacy that you love your children more fully. This "Couple Power" is a stabilizing factor in your child's life.
- Intimacy is a priceless jewel that forms the foundation for your entire family.
- At root, the "home court" philosophy is this: Live the life you want your kids to live.

Home Court Advantage

Practical Suggestions for Family Meals,

Significant Times Together, and More

"What's cookin' tonight?" I often ask Hannah.

That question is part of an ongoing conversation that Sande and I have with Hannah regarding her weekend plans with friends.

"Dad," she replied, "it's only 7:00. We don't even make plans until 9:00 P.M."

Sometimes they don't.

"Why don't you have your friends over, we'll get some pizzas, and you can go in the Jacuzzi?" I asked.

"No," she said, "I don't think we'll do that."

Well, by 9:00 P.M. that evening our living room was full of kids.

We like having Hannah's friends around; they're great. I'm thankful they're here and not hanging around elsewhere. The truth is, I'd rather have Hannah around with a living room full of teenagers (which sometimes sounds like the monkey cage at the local zoo) than have a chronically quiet home and Hannah out with her friends.

If you want "home court" children, you'll quickly pick up on one of the basic rules: The "home" in "home court advantage" means your child should spend a lot of time around your place, whether she's by herself or with dozens of friends.

So what should you do on that home playing field? Here are 10 practical pointers for making the most of your home court advantage.

Pointer 1: Party at Home Sweet Home

For Lauren's 11th birthday party we didn't go to that Cheese-Breath Rodent place. We had a Saturday pool party at our house.

A lot of parents today don't want their children's parties at home. They don't want to set up, and they certainly don't want to deal with chocolate cake mashed into the Berber carpet.

But the truth is that while you may be wiping fingerprints off the wallpaper for a few days after that party, you'll long remember the fun—along with other times you spent together as a family, the ups and downs of life, the sacrifices you made, the joys you shared.

And when that Cheese-Breath Rodent pizza place has turned into a car wash or a Dollar store 10 years down the line, your home will be a place that your kid loves to return to. Each room will be filled with more memories than he or she could ever recount.

What do you want your kids to remember about growing up? When Lauren remembers her birthdays, I want our home to be part of those memories.

Why is that important? If you want "home court" children, you need to nurture their homing instinct.

Home is the primary place where life happens. I'm not much of a poet, but that last sentence may be the most heartwarming sentence I've ever written or ever will write.

Pointer 2: Make Home a Place of Refuge

Lauren was sitting beside me as I watched a *CNN Headline News* story about a man who was on the FBI's Most Wanted list for brutalizing people.

"Can we watch something else?" peeped Lauren, who has the disposition of a butterfly.

Realizing that what she was hearing was a little too much for her 11-year-old ears, I changed the channel. She started to cry and buried her head in my chest.

"What's wrong?" I asked.

"Daddy, I'm afraid," she said. "I'm afraid to fly."

Lauren and Hannah were only weeks away from flying to California to visit their brother for the weekend. She feared something might happen along the way.

You, parent, are your child's psychological blankie. To build in that sense of safety, you must take time out to comfort them as best you know how—even if you don't know the right words to say.

In such situations, defining a younger child's world for her can help. For many 11-year-olds that world consists of family, school, church, the few friends they have, and their pet.

So I went through the list. "Mommy and Daddy are fine," I said. "Your brother's fine. Your sisters are fine and our home here is safe." We talked again about how there *are* people who might try to hurt others, but that the family was safely around her.

Children need the sense of security and stability that comes from knowing Dad and Mom have a plan. "That's why we don't simply drop you off and let you wander around Tucson or the mall by yourself," I told Lauren. "Do you think that Daddy would ever give permission for you to get on that airplane if I didn't think it was safe?" I asked.

"No," she replied. "But it frightens me, Daddy, that Saddam Hussein is going to come here and hurt us."

She was putting together bits and pieces she'd heard on the news. When she heard about the U.S. attack on Baghdad, and Saddam Hussein being on the move every few hours prior to his capture, and car bombs in Israel, it all got blurred together in her mind.

When you take time to sit with your child, help define her world, and demonstrate that you're there to make home a safe place, that comfort makes home the safest place for her to be.

Pointer 3: Be Spontaneous

I'm a lastborn. I'm into fun! I've never been much of a scheduler, either.

That was evident when the producer of one of my shows asked me recently about my "long-range plans" for the program.

"I don't have any long-range plans," I told him. "If the show's working, let's keep on doing it. If it's not, let's think about doing something else or dropping it."

It's not that I'm *against* scheduling; I just believe that sometimes the most effective connections happen when people take things as they come.

Have you ever had a party turn out wonderfully well? Everyone has such a great time that someone says, "Hey, let's do this again next month." So you make plans, invite the same people over—and it's ho-hum at best. You can rarely re-create those special moments, even with the same people in the same place. More often than not, they just happen.

The same is often true with family fun. If you designate a specific night for getting wild and crazy, it can sometimes have the same effect as asking someone to explain a joke's punch line. All the life goes out of it, like a deflated balloon. Life is too spontaneous for a scheduled weekly fun night to work in most homes.

But when you keep your activities to a minimum, you create the environment for spontaneity to happen. That's when home life becomes a wonder. On the spur of the moment, one of the kids will say, "Hey, let's pop some popcorn!"

You say, "What a great idea! Turn the stupid TV off right now and let's make an evening of it."

Then someone wonders what it would be like to watch the corn pop without a lid. So you put the popper in the middle of the living room on a sheet, take the top off, and let that popcorn fly.

You didn't plan it—but you've lived through an experience that will likely be remembered and talked about for years to come.

And it cost you less than renting a video!

Pointer 4: Make It a Team Sport

When our kids were little we played a game called "Huggy Harry." I'd turn out the lights and they'd hide in the house. Then I'd walk down the hallway with a light held under my face so that I looked a little eerie. The kids would make a sound from the rooms they were in and I'd have to find out where they were. They loved it, and screamed with delight.

One of the benefits of escaping the activity trap is focusing on family events rather than individual ones. Nick Stinnett, Ph.D., professor of human development at the University of Alabama, said that "in his 25-year study, which tracked 14,000 families nationwide, he found the happiest families spent time playing board games and card games together."[1]

That isn't to say that Chutes and Ladders or Uno have magical bonding power. The fact that families are enjoying time together makes the difference.

When you take Jimmy to his soccer game, he may have fun passing to Billy and swapping after-game snacks with Andy. But wouldn't you rather he have even more memories of beating Daddy at Yahtzee, landing on Mommy's railroad in Monopoly, and guessing who did what to whom in Clue with his siblings?

Of course, this will require more than dropping Jimmy off at a field. You'll actually have to clear your schedule enough to sit at the table for an hour or two, ignore the telephone, and create a memory.

As a family counselor, I know your child will be greatly affected when he sees you making sacrifices to do things as a family. I don't know why this is, but kids tend not to notice "getting rides." It may take you 30 minutes to do a drop-off for soccer practice; by the time you pick him up, it'll be 60. Your kid will barely notice your inconvenience. But to sit down with him for an hour and play a game—he'll remember that for days, weeks, even a lifetime.

Games aren't the only family times to pursue, of course. Going camping is another possibility that provides special time with the added benefit of few distractions. "Dad is actually going to take us camping!" your children may wonder. "And Mom, who hates camping, is going along with it. Won't it be fun to see Mom in the morning without her makeup on?"

Pointer 5: Live and Talk Your Faith

During the summer the Leman family heads back East to visit the area in western New York where I grew up. One year Hannah decided to work at a camp across the lake there, as what they call a "dish rag."

As the summer wore on, I grew antsy over seeing so little of my daughter. Which is why, when she was getting ready to travel to a week-long youth conference at the end of the summer, I jumped at the chance to drive her to Wal-Mart to pick up a few things before she caught the bus.

After we stopped by the store, I drove Hannah to where the group was gathering for the bus. We had about an hour before she left. We talked; I held her hand and prayed audibly that she would draw closer to God during the coming week, and that she would enjoy her time and return safely.

You might call that "family devotions."

I would.

To me, family devotions have always been the devotion I show to my family. When you show you're devoted to your kids, they'll be drawn to you and your life—including your faith.

We've never had devotions in the typical sense with our children, gathering around the family Bible and reading through it aloud. But acts of love and consideration, reflecting the heart of God, *are* my family devotions. Not only do they show my love for my kids, they also show my love for God without forcing something artificial on them.

That isn't to say a family shouldn't read Scripture together. It just isn't what we've chosen to do. What matters more to me is whether we live our lives in such a way that our kids see our faith is for real.

Ironically, as Hannah and I sat in the parking lot having a wonderful time with each other and with God, one of the women leaders came over and motioned for Hannah to come inside to pray in a circle. Given the choice of being in that circle and sitting outside talking and praying with my daughter whom I hadn't seen much all summer, I chose the latter. That kind of devotion to a child makes the devoted heart of God real to her.

My approach to this subject differs from the one my mom took. When I was a little boy, every morning before school my mother put her arms around me and sang a little song as I went out the door. My friends Moonhead Dietsch and Jamie Huber would watch and roll their eyes.

"Guide and direct us just for today," she would sing, "help us, dear Father, all through the day."

God love her, she tried. But if I hear that song one more time, I'm going to hurl.

When it comes to raising kids with an appreciation for faith in God, I believe in talking with them as opportunities arise, giving them what I call "commercial announcements."

Lauren, for example, watched a TV show with me during Passion Week because I wanted her to revisit the Easter story. "Do you see how hard it is to believe?" I pointed out when Thomas asked to see the holes in Christ's hands.

Another time my mother was near death—doctors had her heart out of her chest at age 80—and I remember pleading to God, "Lord, I have never prayed this hard in my life. I believe my mom has more life in her, if it's Your will." It's important that our kids see us praying at those moments.

Not that it's always easy to talk with our kids about some subjects. After I spoke to a group of adults and youth at a church on the topic of my book *Sex Begins in the Kitchen*, a mom approached me. She asked, "Is the next session going to be so . . . well, you know . . ." She blushed. "Is it going to be like the last one? Because I think it's just *way* too much for my 10-year-old."

"I must disagree with you," I told her. "I can tell you that your 10-year-old is thinking a lot about sex."

"Well, yes," she countered. "But even if he is, that's the home's responsibility to do that."

"Have *you* talked to your son about sex?" I asked.

"Well, no, not yet," she said, then added hastily, "but we're planning on it."

Well, she's two years late already.

Most of us are protective of our kids; we'd like to put them under glass so they don't head down the wrong path or reject our faith. But that isn't going to help prepare them for life. If you want a shot at passing on your spiritual and moral values, live your life genuinely and talk about your faith in God openly and honestly. That's "home court," day-by-day discipleship.

Pointer 6: Togetherness—It's What's for Dinner

The day is always better for me if I walk into the house and smell dinner cooking—not only because the fragrance starts me salivating, but because prime family time at the Leman home has always been around the dinner table.

In a household that takes advantage of the home court, dinner ought to be a time when the family comes together and shares the day's ups and downs.

If your dinner together doesn't last an hour, was it really enough? Do you come together and eat in silence? Do you eat separately—a kind of drive-through fast food service? Are you one of the 33 percent of families that says one parent's late work schedule gets in the way of eating dinner together?[2] Or is dinner a time of relaxing and connecting?

Make the most of dinnertime. There's a strong correlation between "regular family meals and success in school, better psychological adjustment, lower rates of alcohol and drug use and reduced chances of early sexual behavior," as shown by a study of American teens in 2000.[3]

In many homes, kids wolf dinner down, say, "Can I be excused?" if they're respectful, then run to do their homework or get on the Internet or curl up in front of the TV.

That makes for lots of lost opportunities—like telling stories.

My father often told stories at the dinner table. Half the time he'd start laughing before he even got started. Before *we* knew what he was talking about, we'd start laughing, too. I'm sure he embellished a few of the tales—but, boy, they were funny. For instance, he and his friends would take an oil can into a movie theater and pour the stuff down the aisle's rubber mat. Then they'd raise a ruckus in the hope that the manager would come running into the theater—and slip on the oil!

Kids love stories, especially about when you were little. From Day One we've done what I call the Family Fun Confession around the dinner table. Part of it is telling stories about my life that demonstrate to my kids that the challenges and failures they face are the same ones I faced growing up.

If you know something is a struggle for your kids, talk about it on the sly in a story without moralizing. You don't want to give them a week straight of daddy failure stories, but you might sneak one in now and then. Look for their reaction as you talk. "You did *that*, Daddy? You got in trouble for that? You didn't make the team? You got busted?"

You can share more than food with your kids next time you sit down to dinner. You can share your imperfect self with them, too.

Pointer 7: Value Extended Family

I talked with one woman who said her grandmother was "always a birthday card and a $20 bill at Christmas."

How sad. Even if miles separate the kids from the grandparents, which is often the case today, it's too bad that grandchild didn't try to make the best of the situation by tapping into her grandmother's world.

All too soon, grandmas are gone. The child who didn't know Grandma won't know anything about the lady's history, where the family came from, or what his own roots are. It's harder to really know your own "home" court when that happens.

My advice to young families is to live near one set of parents. That means prioritizing your life around people, not things. Long-distance relationships tend to lose intimacy. You may do your best to keep up through e-mailed digital photos, audio or video recordings shipped back and forth, letters, phone calls, and visits. Those all help, but they aren't the same as living in the same community.

It's a tough reality that many of us today don't live in our parents' time zones. My mother is closer to our children than to her other grandchildren simply because she lives in our town. As much as we might like to say it's possible to make up the difference when we give up regular, face-to-face, personal contact, that simply isn't possible. If you want the full benefit of your extended family in raising your children, living near each other is essential.

Extended family can be such an integral part of your children's lives. My kids remember the songs Grandma sang to them. Kevin II remembers how, when he wanted to join in the painting at his grandparents' house, Grandma let him "paint" her wall with water while the grown-ups painted the rest of the house. Having relatives nearby gives your children a foundation of memories, indelible imprints like yours that bind them to family.

Pointer 8: Chip In Creatively

How many kids see the electric bill on the counter and pay any attention to it? One way to help kids feel they're part of the family is to make them partly accountable for the bottom line on utility bills every month.

On the surface that doesn't sound the least bit exciting. But I'd approach it this way. You might say during dinner one night, "You know, I've been thinking. This family needs to have more fun. This family needs more pizza, more movies, and more trips to the bowling alley." Tap into whatever interests the family has; no kid is going to take issue with that.

"However much you all can save on these bills month by month over last year will go into a pot. Then we'll blow the whole wad on bowling, pizza, and family movies—whatever."

That's a fun and practical alternative to barking out, "Hey, what's the front door doing open? What do you think we're doing, heating the neighborhood?"

Have a good time as a family charting the history of how many kilowatts you used last year and what you spent. Many bills come with such comparisons graphed out; if not, have your kids graph these out themselves. As they assume responsibility for use of electricity, gas, and water, they'll feel they're part of the action—and part of the family.

You don't get kids to feel they belong by stopping outside activities and declaring, "Okay, now we all belong to each other! We're just going to love, love, love!" Pretty soon those kids will be killing each other. Instead, let them be part of the vacation-planning process. Or if Dad spends $7 every Friday to have his car washed, give the kids the opportunity to do it themselves. That $7 can go toward much more important expenditures—Canadian bacon and pineapple pizza, to name one.

Pointer 9: Try "Stay at Home with Your Kids" Day

Do you know what your kids are doing after school, on the Internet, or alone in their rooms? If not, it may be due to "cocooning." Dad comes home from work, and after dinner he plants himself in front of *Monday Night Football.* The kids slip into their rooms and go online or play video games.

In too many homes, parents and kids live in separate cocoons. It shouldn't be that way in a "home court" family. If you want to enter your child's world, try "Stay at Home with Your Kids" Day.

You're probably familiar with "Take Your Kids to Work" Day. I've done that kind of thing, pulling my kids out of school to visit the radio studio or taking them with me on a business trip over a weekend. It gives us an opportunity to focus on each other and talk about life, and it lets them see exactly what I do. It's a great idea; whether you're a stuntman or a librarian, your kids will love the adventure.

But it's just as important—if not more—to get into your kid's world. Do you know what TV shows your daughter watches when she comes home from school? Do you know where your son takes the dog after he drops his books on his bed? If you work outside the home, you may have no idea.

To combat this, try taking a personal day off work and stay at home with your kid. Tune into what he or she is doing.

If you can't get a personal day, see if you can put in extra hours for a week or two. Then take a half day and come home before your school-aged child gets there. Or schedule it on a Saturday.

Why? Because the day will come, sooner than you can imagine, when you'll be waving good-bye to your child as he or she enters adulthood. Tears will be streaming down your face; you'll be thinking, *Where did the time go?*

On that day, if someone offered to take you back in time to spend an entire day with your kid when she was three or eight or sixteen, you'd do it in a heartbeat—even if it cost you a thousand dollars. Do it now, when all it will cost you is a day off work.

If you have more than one child, you might spend time with one in the morning and another in the afternoon. However many kids you have, I recommend spending time with them one-on-one. If you have a houseful, you'll need to arrange a few of these days.

Plan an activity, preferably at home, that your kids would love. Play her favorite board game; work on that model he's building; play catch in the backyard; learn the secrets of his favorite video game; go to her favorite Web sites.

If you don't know what to do, let your kid assume the role of teacher. Say something like, "You know, it's funny. I really have no idea what you do when you come home from school. Would you show me how you get your friends online to chat?"

Another option is to take a day trip. Pack a surprise lunch for each other. Talk about your lives. Choose an activity that allows you to converse—not a movie. Pull out an old photo album. As you look at those pictures, talk about what your feelings were about life at that point, what you loved and feared.

You may be opening the door for teachable moments—like the time Lauren and I were listening to a country radio station. The DJ said, "Forty-five percent of single men say they have done this on vacation. What is it?" People called in with various answers, but the answer was "Have a one-night stand."

Lauren looked over to me and asked innocently, "What's a one-night stand?"

My explanation gave us the opportunity to talk about the sanctity of marriage, the reality of sexually transmitted diseases, and the strength of her own parents' marriage—topics neither of us had any way of knowing would come up.

Pointer 10: Spread the "Home Court" Philosophy

You may pull your child out of the activity trap, but if other families on your block are still caught, the neighborhood can be a pretty dead place. The solution isn't to march over to the neighbors and demand that they drop their activities. Set an example with your own choices. Draw other kids to your home through your activities; don't wrestle them out of theirs.

Giving your son some spare lumber so that he and the kids down the street can build a tree fort behind your house, for instance, might make your home a pretty cool place to be. That will be more likely to happen, of course, if you get to know the other parents.

Don't think for a moment that they're not watching. I know one mother who was won over to homeschooling when she realized that all the kids she wanted her daughter to hang around with were home-schooled. She didn't respond to a sermon, a lesson, or speeches over the backyard fence about how parents who "really" love their kids wouldn't *think* about sending them to "godless, secular" schools. She just watched and made up her own mind.

That was also the case with an editor who stopped by our house for dinner once. He was overwhelmed by the experience. He saw our adult kids excited about seeing each other, bantering around the table. "Dr. Leman," he said, "most parents would give their right arm to have a family like this. How did you do it?"

The funny thing is, he should have known—he's worked on several of my books! But I just told him, "If you make home a meaningful, loving, and fun place while they're growing up, the kids will want to return to it again and again and again."

Some of our neighbors, meanwhile, have wondered why we sometimes make such a scene saying good-bye to our older children: "Do you really have to act as if the *Titanic* has just sunk every time they're going away?"

"We love each other so much that it *feels* like the *Titanic* has sunk," I say, without apology. I can see the envy in their eyes.

The Home Court Advantage

You can never guarantee how your children will turn out. I've seen fantastic people who were raised by the most inept, incompetent parents I've ever laid eyes on. And I've seen some very godly parents go through years of heartbreak with a rebellious son or daughter.

So, while I can't give you any guarantee, I can tell you the odds favor the home court advantage. Chances are that "home court" kids will say no to the worst things in life and eagerly embrace the best.

Kids with the home court advantage have a place where they're noticed, trained, appreciated, encouraged, and loved. By and large, they'll become winners. They may not all run for President or become CEOs, but they're likely to have successful, fulfilling, meaningful lives.

Kids who are merely kept busy will face a number of crises when the busyness stops. If they've never been bored at home, they may fear boredom at college and rush into drugs, alcohol, or premarital sex. If they haven't been taught how to handle failure, how to be gracious in success, how to belong, how to cooperate (instead of always trying to win), the real world will be a tough place, a tempting place, and a scary place.

Give your kids the home court advantage. Send them out with the best chance of success: a sense of belonging, a certainty that they come from a place where they were, are, and always will be deeply loved and welcomed.

Let's Remember:

- The "home" in "home court advantage" means your child should spend a lot of time around your home, whether she's by herself or with friends.
- Try to host many of your family celebrations at home to help build emotional attachment as a family—as well as to the house itself as a place of memories.
- Home should be a refuge. To build a sense of safety in your kids, take time to comfort them as well as you know how.
- Designating a specific "family fun night" can have the same effect as asking someone to explain a joke's punch line. Keep planned activities to a minimum, creating the environment for more spontaneous family fun.
- Let your kids see that when life throws you curve balls, you handle them through prayer and by talking with your spouse. When you show you're devoted to your family, your children will be drawn to you and your faith.
- Dinner ought to be one of the primary times when the family comes together and shares the ups and downs of the day.
- Extended family members are an integral part of your children's lives. My advice to young families is to live near one set of par-

ents, which will mean prioritizing your life around people and not things.

- One of the ways to help kids feel a part of the family is to make them partly accountable for the bottom line on utility bills. You can then use the savings to bankroll family fun.

- Try "Stay at Home with Your Kids" Day. Take a personal day off work and stay home with your child to enter his or her world. Use it as an opportunity to have fun and to use the teachable moments that may arise.

- Set a countercultural example in your neighborhood through your "home court" choices. Draw neighborhood kids to your home with your activities; don't wrestle them out of theirs.

Epilogue

My 60th Birthday Party

I had it all figured out.

Throughout the summer I'd been listening for clues from the kids. From the snatches of conversation I'd overheard, I gathered there was going to be a big party for my 60th birthday.

The family hadn't said this explicitly, of course, but that only whetted my anticipation. The closest anyone came to letting any secret plans slip was Krissy, when she said to me, "You have the big 6-0 coming. We're really going to have to do *that* one up right."

We'd certainly done my brother Jack's 60th birthday up right. When *he* turned the big 6-0, there had been a huge party; we'd gone to Sacramento to surprise him. Our family knows how to throw a proper shindig, and my turn was just around the corner.

Or so I thought.

I love birthday parties. I love surprises. Most of all, I love the family gathering together for a good party. I was gearing up for a big one, perhaps the biggest one of all.

My birthday would fall on Labor Day, which couldn't have been more ideal for family and friends to converge over the weekend. I couldn't have planned it better if I'd scheduled the day of my own birth. I was ready for fireworks, for a Tucson parade with fire trucks and baton-twirling, and tuba-tooting high school marching bands. I was ready to celebrate!

Labor Day morning finally came. I thought, *All right. Where's Kevin?* His arrival from Burbank, California, was the only piece still left in my birthday puzzle, and would confirm my suspicions.

But as every hour passed, I became more confused at the seeming lack of family activity. Morning came and went and family members were barely out of bed. Afternoon came and went and everyone seemed to be walking in slow motion. Evening came—but Kevin didn't.

I couldn't help myself. I finally had to ask. "Isn't Kevin coming over today?"

"No, honey, I'm sorry. He couldn't make it. But I'm sure he'll call."

Kevin's not coming? I thought. *Burbank is only a 45-minute plane ride from Tucson. He's not coming on my* birthday?

On any other day, I would have said we had a great evening with a relaxed dinner at home—finished off by a birthday cake. Sande, Holly, Hannah, and Lauren were there, along with Krissy and her husband, Dennis.

Hey, I reasoned, *when you're on the road as much as I am, it's nice to have a quiet dinner at home.* But to me, it was as gray a birthday as could be. I couldn't shake my disappointment.

Sande will tell you that I whined and complained all week about the fact that my son didn't visit. It was undoubtedly one of the longest weeks of her life.

The following Friday evening, I was told that the family was going out to dinner—but that Holly was running a bit late. In fact, she was right on schedule. Following a secret plan, she was driving to the airport to pick up my brother and sister-in-law, who'd flown in from California. When the three of them walked into the restaurant, I knew everyone had pulled a good one over on me!

It only got better from there.

Next morning Jack and I were at the house when Sande called from an errand in town. "Honey," she said in that tempting, singsong tone, "why don't you come down to the Eclectic and have breakfast with me and Linda? They've got that $1.99 special."

Jack and I drove down. As I sat in a booth with my menu, deciding on my order, a voice behind me asked, "What would you like to drink?"

"Coffee," I replied without turning around.

"*Coffee?*" he said. "That's *all* you want is *coffee?*"

Who is this brash kid talking to me like that? I thought as I spun around.

Looking up, I saw my son, Kevin II, beaming. After doing a double take, I was so elated to see him that I slammed my fist on the table and yelled. Everyone in the restaurant turned. It was as if I'd pulled the plug on every conversation.

But holey-kamoley! My son was in town! Five days late, but, hey— better late than never, right?

The party came the next day, when they whisked me away to the local country club. Fifty or sixty guests were waiting: family, close friends, coworkers, and folks I'd known since I was a boy. I also received wonderful letters from friends and colleagues all over the country: Chuck Swindoll, Jim Dobson, Neil Clark Warren, Gary Smalley, and Les and Leslie Parrott. I couldn't have gathered a better bunch of people if I'd made the list myself.

In this day and age, I thought as I watched my kids interact with the guests throughout the dinner, *when kids use four-letter words with their parents and view reward as their right, Sande and I are fortunate to have kids who care so much about other people.*

Holly, the firstborn leader of the clan, got up immediately after the dinner and introduced herself to many guests. She knew some of these people hadn't seen others in quite some time and might feel a bit uncomfortable. Watching her thoughtfully "work" the room, I kept thinking, *Look at that daughter of yours, Leman. Just like a fairy tale: "As good as she is beautiful." Could you have asked for any more?*

Many guests later remarked on how different our kids seemed from "most kids."

But what was most special to me happened at the evening's close. Each family member stood and shared words that would have touched the heart of any husband and father.

Holly, an English teacher with a great command of the language and the compassionate heart of her mother, gave a beautiful tribute. She talked about how, now that she's older, she appreciates much more the sacrifices Sande and I made.

"He's always had a great sense of humor," said Kevin II. "But, most importantly, he modeled what a man is and what a husband is."

"I love you," said Lauren. "And you write really good books with interesting titles—although I've never read any of them."

Krissy shared about the importance of family. She told how, after speaking to a group of CEOs in Mexico City, I said to Sande, "Why don't we fly to Chicago and say hi to Krissy?" Changing our plane reservations, we flew to Chicago with two Mexican sombreros and serapes, which we wore to our daughter's dorm and surprised her.

When Sande got up and said, "He's the squashiest," I began to cry as if on cue.

But Hannah stole the show without even knowing it.

After beginning by using the same words another speaker had used a few minutes earlier, causing all of us to laugh uproariously, she turned serious. "I love my dad," she said as her voice quavered and she fumbled for words. "And I couldn't ask for a better dad."

That pretty much summed it up, but then something unexpected happened. She began to cry. "Oh," she said as tears streamed down her face and she fanned them with her hand. "What's happening here?"

When she said that, looking for all the world like her mother, tears again blurred my vision.

Hannah, I thought as I answered her in my heart, *what's happening to you is life. You're 16 years old and you're thinking about all the wonderful times we've had together as a family. You're just beginning to think about college and about leaving home, and it's hitting you that your daddy's 60 years old already and that you're not going to have him around forever. You're also realizing on a deeper level that we have loved you just as you are, and that the love that we share and the priority that we all place on family is priceless.*

Honey, the tears flowing down your cheeks come from the same place as the ones flowing down mine—from that deep, deep bond we share together. That's what's happening.

Some say you can't go home again. They mean the home you grew up in will never be quite the same place it used to be. But no relationship is static, and no past perfectly preserved. The question is, what do you want your home to become?

You *can* go home. You *must* turn home if you want that home court advantage for your children, and the deepening relationships that come from shared lives.

It may seem that your child will never grow up, but the truth is that life really is short. My brother Jack and I asked each other recently, "Of all the days we both have left in this life, how many of them will we spend doing something together? Thirty? Sixty? Ninety if we're fortunate?" We just don't know, and neither of us is getting any younger.

Likewise, how many days do we have with our kids? Those, too, are numbered. I just want a shot at making a difference in my kids' lives while we still have days together at home.

Soon Hannah probably will be heading off to college. As I said to her one afternoon, "You know Dad. When you leave, I'll be standing in the front yard bawling my eyes out."

The *Titanic* will sink one more time!

Sande and I know that Lauren's day to leave the nest won't be far behind. But even as our last child heads down Tourmaline Drive and we're left blubbering in the driveway, we'll know this: The time, energy, care, and love we've poured into our kids' lives means that seeing them off is not the end.

The blessing of those relationships is that they'll continue to deepen as our kids head into the world—most likely getting married and having children of their own, as Krissy and Dennis did recently. The beauty of having "home court" children is that they mature into the kind of adults you can be friends with the rest of your life.

So, what creates that home court advantage for your kids?

Love.

Discipline.

Positive, healthy expectations.

The belief that who they are is more important than anything they could ever do.

True devotion, lived out in the everyday arena of life.

Knowing that the whole of the family is more important than its parts.

If we're married, being committed as spouses for life—mates who make their relationship a top priority.

Downtime.

A sense of belonging.

These are the ingredients we've poured into our family. That 60th birthday party told me that Sande and I must have gotten something right, because it sure tasted sweet to me.

When I look back at all we've invested in raising Holly, Krissy, Kevin II, Hannah, and Lauren—would I do it all over again?

In a heartbeat.

Notes

Chapter 1

1. Proverbs 22:6.
2. G. Jeffrey MacDonald, "Smarter Toys, Smarter Tots?" *The Christian Science Monitor* online, August 20, 2003 (www.csmonitor .com/2003/0820/p12s02-lifp.html).
3. Jon Sarche, Associated Press, "Pilot, 7, On Flight Across U.S., Is Killed When Plane Crashes—Girl's Father, Instructor, Also Dies Near Wyo. Airport," *Seattle Times* online, April 11, 1996
4. MacDonald, "Smarter Toys, Smarter Tots?" *The Christian Science Monitor* online.
5. Ibid.
6. Brenda Hunter, Ph.D., *Home by Choice: Raising Emotionally Secure Children in an Insecure World* (Sisters, Ore.: Multnomah Press, 2000), p. 41. Quoting John Bowlby, *Separation: Anxiety and Anger*, vol. 2 of *Attachment and Loss* (New York: Basic Books, 1980), p. 204.
7. William J. Bennett, *The Index of Leading Cultural Indicators: Facts and Figures on the State of American Society* (New York: Simon and Schuster, 1994), pp. 102-103.
8. Claudia Wallis, "The Case for Staying Home," *Time* (March 22, 2004), p. 52.
9. Amelia Warren Tyagi, "Why Women Have to Work," *Time* (March 22, 2004), p. 56.

10. Sonja Steptoe, "Ready, Set, Relax!" *Time* (October 27, 2003), p. 38.

Chapter 2

1. Bruce Stockler, A. J. Jacobs, and Andy Ward, "The Hurried Man," *Esquire* (February 2003), pp. 80-83.
2. Lisa Collier Cool, "Back to School 2001: The Overwhelmed Child," *Good Housekeeping* (August 2001), pp. 79-82.
3. Greg Toppo, "Teens with Multiple Choices Make Surprising One," *USA Today*, August 6, 2003, p. D5.
4. George Barna, *Real Teens* (Ventura, Calif.: Regal Books, 2001), p. 71.
5. Sam Kashner, "Producing the Producers," *Vanity Fair* (January 2004), p. 105.

Chapter 3

1. David Noonan, "Stop Stressing Me," *Newsweek* (January 29, 2001), p. 54.

Chapter 5

1. Cesar G. Soriano, "For Babies Who Have Everything," *USA Today*, January 12, 2004 (www.usatoday.com/life/lifestyle/2004-01-12-baby-shower-gifts_x.htm).
2. 1 Timothy 6:10.

Chapter 6

1. Doug Grow, "Special School Crowns a Special King," *Star Tribune*, October 4, 2003, pp. B1, 5.
2. "Routine Builds Family Health," *USA Today*, December 10, 2002, p. D9.

Chapter 7

1. "Opie the Birdman," original air date September 30, 1963, Episode 101, *The Andy Griffith Show,* Mayberry Enterprises, Inc., 1963.
2. "Mr. McBeevee," original air date October 1, 1962, Episode 64, *The Andy Griffith Show,* Mayberry Enterprises, Inc., 1961.

Chapter 8

1. Robert Kurson, "Just Another Father-Son Story," *Esquire* (November 2002), pp. 160-168.
2. Lisa Collier Cool, "Back to School 2001: The Overwhelmed Child," *Good Housekeeping* (August 2001), p. 80.
3. Psalm 23:4.
4. Sylvia Krista Smith, "Gwyneth in Love," *Vanity Fair* (February 2004), p. 151.
5. Donna Freydkin, "Paltrow Finds a New Peace," *USA Today,* October 14, 2003, pp. D1-2.
6. Ibid., p. D1.
7. Ibid., p. D2.
8. Luke 15:11-32.

Chapter 9

1. Marilee Jones, "Parents Get Too Aggressive on Admissions," *USA Today,* January 6, 2003, p. A13.
2. Ibid.
3. Jane Gross, "Exposing the Cheat Sheet, with the Students' Aid," *The New York Times,* November 26, 2003, p. A26.
4. Ibid.
5. L. Lamor Williams, "Getting a Jump on College Ways: Students at Arlington School Gain Discipline to Work on Their Own," *Star-Telegram* online (April 24, 2004).

6. Found online at http://www.graceprep.org/.
7. John Cloud and Jodie Morse, "Home Sweet School," *Time* (August 27, 2001), pp. 46-54.

Chapter 10

1. Found online at http://www.businessweek.com/bwdaily/dnflash/ aug2001/nf20010828_616.htm.
2. Ron Suskind, "Mrs. Hughes Takes Her Leave," *Esquire* (July 2002), p. 103.
3. Ibid., pp. 100-107, 110.

Chapter 11

1. Mary Elizabeth Williams, "The Working Mother's Survival Guide," *Parents* (June 2003), p. 60.
2. Terence P. Jeffrey, "Stand Up If You Would Rather Be Raised by a Daycare Worker," *Human Events* (June 18, 2001), pp. 12-13.
3. Anita Sethi, "The Daycare Dilemma," *Baby Talk* (November 2003), pp. 17-18.
4. Found online at http://www.spencerandwaters.com/calculate.html.
5. Hunter, *Home by Choice: Raising Emotionally Secure Children in an Insecure World*, p. 33.
6. Kim Masters, "Working vs. Staying Home: Why We Judge Other Moms . . . and How to Make Peace with Your *Own* Choice," *Parenting* (May 2003), p. 132.
7. Claudia Wallis, "The Case for Staying Home," *Time* (March 22, 2004), p. 52.
8. U.S. Census Bureau, as quoted in *Newsweek* (May 17, 2004), p. E2.
9. Hunter, *Home by Choice: Raising Emotionally Secure Children in an Insecure World*, p. 35.

10. Ibid., p. 36.
11. Douglas Carlton Abrams, "Father Nature: The Making of a Modern Dad," *Psychology Today* (March/April 2002), p. 38.
12. Eve Heyn, "The Daddy Track," *Parenting* (September 2003), p. 152.
13. Abrams, "Father Nature: The Making of a Modern Dad," *Psychology Today*, pp. 38-47.
14. Ibid., p. 44.

Chapter 13

1. Cindy Schweich Handler, "Be a Ready Parent," *Redbook* (April 2001), p. 182.

Chapter 14

1. Anna Quindlen, "Doing Nothing Is Something," *Newsweek* (May 13, 2002), p. 76.
2. Katherine Lee, "Why Babies Need Downtime," *Parenting* (March 2003), p. 85.
3. Ibid.
4. Dr. David Elkins, "The Overbooked Child: Are We Pushing Our Kids Too Hard?" *Psychology Today* (January/February 2003), pp. 64, 66.

Chapter 15

1. Mike Mason, *The Mystery of Marriage* (Sisters, Ore.: Multnomah Books, 1985), p. 124.

Chapter 16

1. Charlotte Latvala, "8 Secrets of Happy Families," *Parenting* (October 2002), pp. 105-106.

2. "Late Hours Biggest Barrier to Family Dining," *USA Today*, November 11, 2003, p. A1.
3. Karen S. Peterson, "Extracurricular Burnout," *USA Today*, November 19, 2002, p. D7.

enjoy the **journey**™

Does parenting sometimes seem like an overwhelming task? Your role as a parent is difficult but very important to you and your children, and Focus on the Family® wants to encourage you! The complimentary Focus on Your Child® membership program has age-specific materials that provide timely encouragement, advice and information for today's busy parents. With newsletters or audio journals delivered straight to your doorstep once a month and a Web site packed with over 900 articles, Focus on Your Child can help you enjoy the journey!

Here's what the membership includes:

Parenting Newsletters: Four age-specific and concise editions for parents with no spare time.

Audio Journals: Timely information for parents and fun activities for children, based on their ages.

Online Resources: Age-customized articles, e-mail news, recommended resources and topic-organized forum through which parents can share with one another.

To sign up, go to www.focusonyourchild.com or call (800) A-FAMILY.

For information regarding speaking availability, business consultations, or seminars, please contact Dr. Leman at:

Dr. Kevin Leman
P.O. Box 35370
Tucson, Arizona 85740
Phone (520) 797-3830
Fax (520) 797-3809
Web sites: www.realfamilies.com
www.matchwise.com

Books by Dr. Kevin Leman:

Becoming the Parent God Wants You to Be
Becoming a Couple of Promise
The Birth Order Book
A Chicken's Guide to Talking Turkey to Your Kids about Sex
First Time Mom
Keeping Your Family Strong in a World Gone Wrong
Living in a Stepfamily without Getting Stepped On
Making Children Mind without Losing Yours
Making Sense of the Men in Your Life
My Firstborn, There's No One Like You
My Middle Child, There's No One Like You
My Lastborn, There's No One Like You
My Only Child, There's No One Like You
The Perfect Match

The Real You: Becoming the Person You Were Meant To Be
Running the Rapids: Guiding Teenagers through the Turbulent Waters of Adolescence
Say Goodbye to Stress
Sex Begins in the Kitchen
Sheet Music: Uncovering the Secrets of Sexual Intimacy in Marriage
Single Parenting That Works!
Ten Secrets to Raising Sensible, Successful Kids
Unlocking the Secrets of Your Childhood Memories
The Way of the Shepherd
What a Difference a Daddy Makes
When Your Best Is Not Good Enough
Women Who Try Too Hard

Video series:

Bringing Peace and Harmony to the Blended Family
Making Children Mind without Losing Yours (Christian—parenting edition)
Making Children Mind without Losing Yours (Secular—public school teacher edition)

Making the Most of Marriage
Running the Rapids: Guiding Teenagers through the Turbulent Waters of Adolescence
Single Parenting That Works!